MEN

AT THE CROSSROADS

Beyond
Traditional Roles
& Modern Options

JACK BALSWICK

INTERVARSITY PRESS
DOWNERS GROVE, ILLINOIS 60515

InterVarsity Press® is the book-publishing division of InterVarsity Christian Fellowship®, a student movement active on campus at hundreds of universities, colleges and schools of nursing in the United States of America, and a member movement of the International Fellowship of Evangelical Students. For information about local and regional activities, write Public Relations Dept., InterVarsity Christian Fellowship, 6400 Schroeder Rd., P.O. Box 7895, Madison, WI 53707-7895.

Scripture quotations, unless otherwise noted, are from the New Revised Standard Version of the Bible, copyright 1989 by the Division of Christian Education of the National Council of the Churches of Christ in the U.S.A. and are used by permission.

Cover illustration: Roberta Polfus

ISBN 0-8308-1385-3

Printed in the United States of America ∞

Library of Congress Cataloging-in-Publication Data

Balswick, Jack O.
  Men at the crossroads: beyond traditional roles and modern
options/by Jack Balswick.
    p.   cm.
  Includes bibliographical references.
  ISBN 0-8308-1385-3
  1. Men—United States.   2. Men—United States—Psychology.
3. Masculinity (Psychology)—United States.   4. Men—United States—
Religious life.   I. Title.
HQ1090.3.B355   1992
305.31—dc20   92-20599
                                                                  CIP

17	16	15	14	13	12	11	10	9	8	7	6	5	4	3	2	1
05	04	03	02	01	00	99	98	97	96	95	94	93	92			

Acknowledgments _____ 7

PART I: INTRODUCTION _____ 9

1 **Men in Difficult Times:** *Who Stole My Script?* _____ 11

PART II: IN SEARCH OF THE REAL MALE _____ 21

2 **Why Are Men Different from Women?** *The Traditional
Male and the Feminist Challenge* _____ 23
3 **The New Male:** *King, Warrior, Magician and Lover* _____ 38
4 **The Christian Male:** *A Radical Alternative* _____ 49

PART III: MALE ISSUES _____ 63

5 **Male Inexpressiveness:** *Barrier to Intimacy* _____ 65
6 **Competition, Aggression and War:** *Restraining the Warrior* ___ 78
7 **Men, Power and Control:** *From Intimidation to Empowering* ___ 87
8 **Male Sexuality:** *Releasing the Lover* _____ 100
9 **Male Spirituality:** *Renewing the Spirit* _____ 120
10 **Stages of a Man's Life:** *Growing Through Crisis* _____ 134

PART IV: MEN IN RELATIONSHIPS _____ 151

11 **Fathering:** *Reestablishing the Vital Connection* _____ 153
12 **Male Friendships:** *Finding Our Brothers* _____ 172
13 **Friendships with Women:** *I Want a Sister, Not a Sweetheart* ___ 187

PART V: CONCLUSION _____ 201

14 **Men Made New:** *Beyond Traditional Roles and
Modern Options* _____ 203
References _____ 215

Acknowledgments

The ideas presented in this book have formed over the last twenty-five years as I have been involved in "men's issues." I am grateful to Gary Sattler, my co-teacher of the course "Men in Difficult Times" at Fuller Seminary. Students in my various classes have also contributed to my understanding of men during my twenty-eight years of teaching. I thank several of my students—Stephen Carey, Philip Moore, Marc Nord, Barbara Oostdyk, Brad Stenberg and Michael Webb—who offered helpful suggestions for portions of this book. Rodney Clapp and Ruth Goring Stewart have also provided most generous and valuable editorial assistance.

I dedicate this book to my son Joel and grandsons Curtis and Jacob, who I hope will find as complete a model of Christian manhood in me as I was fortunate enough to find in my father, Orville, and grandfathers Alvin and Peter.

PART I

INTRODUCTION

———

1

MEN IN DIFFICULT TIMES

Who Stole My Script?

> All the world's a stage,
> And all the men and women merely players;
> They have their exits and their entrances,
> And one man in his time plays many parts,
> His acts being seven ages.
>
> WILLIAM SHAKESPEARE, *AS YOU LIKE IT*

I magine the anxiety of an actor who walks out on stage and suddenly discovers that he cannot remember vital lines that belong to his role. Changing definitions of masculinity have brought many men a similar anxiety in their daily lives.

Take Bill for example. Bill, a twenty-five-year-old computer analyst, has asked Sue for a date. After spending Saturday afternoon washing and polishing his car, he arrives at Sue's apartment to pick her up. The ride to the restaurant is filled with enjoyable talk about similar interests. As he parks and they walk down the street to the restaurant, Bill suddenly realizes that he is walking on the inside of the sidewalk. Should he tactfully slide around to the street side? Will Sue interpret this as patronizing or chauvinistic? What should he do?

As they approach the restaurant door, he steps ahead and gallantly holds the door open for her. Again, he wonders how this act will be interpreted. He wishes there were a clearer script for being a male.

Burt and Nancy have been married for five years and now have two children, ages two and four. Nancy cares for the kids at home while Burt works full-time in an office. As Burt enters the house after a busy day, he kicks off his shoes, turns on the radio and reads the evening paper while Nancy busily prepares the evening meal. Burt suddenly realizes how "traditional" this is and wonders whether Nancy is resentful because he isn't helping with the meal. He has no clear script for being a husband.

The next day Burt goes shopping for Christmas gifts. He selects a doll for little Heather and a baseball glove for his son, Jacob. As he is about to pay for his purchases, he suddenly wonders whether his gifts are reinforcing sexist stereotypes in his children. Confused, he's not sure what to do.

In past times, men were guided by a clearly defined male script. This script was clear, especially because it complemented a clearly defined female script that any woman could follow. In a world where "men were men and women were women," there was little gender-role confusion.

Today it's much harder to figure out what a "real man" does and is. In the face of secular challenges, many Christians are tempted to push for a return to the traditional male role as embodying the Christian ideal. But I think that's not a good enough solution. Although the traditional male role contains much that's commendable, we need to search for a *Christian* model of manhood.

The Misunderstood Male

The question of what it means to be a man has only recently surfaced. Throughout most of history it was taken for granted that men acted like men because that was their nature, and women acted like women because they were made that way. Only after the social and behavioral sciences emerged have we begun to question the notion that physiology alone is responsible for sexual temperament and behavior. Crosscultural research has led social scientists to conclude that culture rather than nature is the major determinant of temperamental differences between the genders.

And today, cultural change means that many of us are not exactly sure what it means to be a man. As boys most of us learned a traditional image of manhood that has formed the basis of our masculine identity. As traditional definitions of gender roles have been called into question, though, we find that we're sometimes criticized for being who we were taught to be and doing what we were taught to do. We began the ball game with clearly defined and understood rules, but halfway through the game the rules changed.

Not surprisingly, we're confused. If we behave like traditional males we're called insensitive, chauvinistic, paternalistic, condescending or even sexist. Disliking these labels, many of us have entered a period of soul searching or consciousness raising, exploring not only our attitudes toward women but also our feelings and beliefs about men and masculinity.

The Liberation of the American Male

In these difficult times of gender identity change, men as well as women need to be liberated. When I tell others that I'm involved in the men's liberation movement, I often receive a bewildered look, followed by one of several types of comments. Many women and men ask, "What do men need to be liberated from?" Some women retort, "That's just like men, trying to capitalize on a good thing women started. Why, you're just trying to draw the attention away from us and back to yourselves." Some men give an enthusiastic endorsement: "It's about time; this women's liberation thing has gone too far!" Unfortunately, none of these responses reveals a genuine understanding of men's liberation.

In reality, women and men's roles are two sides of the same coin; one can't be defined without the other. Each is defined by its opposite—and it's impossible to redefine one role without redefining the other. But in fact, this is exactly what our society has been attempting to do since the beginning of the women's movement.

As we call the female role into question, we are automatically questioning what it means to be a male. While women have sought liberation to participate equally in society, men seek liberation from an *internal* bondage.

The traditional definition of the male role is like an emotional strait-jacket that constricts men's development. Among the most binding aspects of the traditional male role are restrictions on feeling and expressing emotions, a fear of being a sissy or acting too feminine, an emphasis on task achievement as proof of self-worth, compulsive competitiveness, a façade of toughness, the desire to be a big wheel, the obligation to be a sturdy oak, and the need to protect one's honor and stand up for one's own rights. At its heart, the men's movement calls for a new definition of manhood that will free men from these restrictions.

A Movement in Reaction

The men's movement is in part a reaction to the women's movement, and because it is, we need to recognize the three stages the women's movement has gone through.

The earliest stage of the women's movement was *assimilation*. Women had become conscious of their economic and political disfranchisement in a male-dominated society. So the goal women set for themselves was simply to prove that they too could be successful in the "rational"—that they could participate in the competitive worlds of business and politics.

Although many women did prove to themselves and others that they were tough enough to compete directly with men, they began to wonder if they had not sacrificed their womanhood in the process. The shortcomings of assimilation led then to the *androgynous* stage, which called women to take the best from ideal masculinity *(andro-)* and ideal femininity *(-gyny)* and incorporate both into existing social structures. In practice, this meant that women should be allowed to create their own roles in institutions that had traditionally been monopolized by men. And in a female-dominated institution such as the family, the goal was increased participation by the father. Rather than being assimilated into the social structures dominated by the opposite sex, men were to participate in them as men, and women as women; the result would be the creation of androgynous social structures.

As a consequence of the androgynous approach, much research was generated to demonstrate how the worlds of work and home have been dehumanizing because they are dominated by one sex. It was shown that the competitive, impersonal workplace was producing anxiety, fatigue, ulcers, career burnout and midlife crises; meanwhile, children were suffering because they had been deprived of their father's nurturing.

Although the androgynous approach has brought about some needed social corrections, when carried to its logical extreme it leads to a blurring of gender distinctives. As I shall point out in the next chapter, some radical feminists and early spokesmen for the men's movement have trumpeted the advantages of a unisex world in which all distinctions between masculinity and femininity would be eradicated. This notion has not gained much support, however, even among the leaders of the popular new men's movement. Instead, the men's movement, along with many feminists, is ushering in the *differentiation* stage. Although recognizing value in the androgynous approach, this view recognizes fundamental differences between males and females. As we shall see in chapter four, the differentiation goal of the men's and women's movements meshes rather well with a Christian view of masculinity and femininity.

The Cost of Rejecting Change
There may have been a time when the traditional male role worked. But given the realities of modern life, trying to perpetuate the old roles is costly. The costs can be tallied in a number of different areas.

The costs to men. The traditional definitions of masculinity may be most costly for males themselves, because they end up forfeiting the potential for richer and fuller lives. The personal tragedy of males' inability to express their feelings was illustrated clearly to me one Saturday afternoon when my wife and I went to see a film version of Shakespeare's *Romeo and Juliet.* The two main characters were being played by sixteen-year-old youths; thus, the matinee performance was crowded with high-school students. At the tragic death scene, my wife and I had lumps in our throats and tears in our eyes, and we heard many girls around us sniffing as well—but there were loud guffaws from the adolescent boys. Obviously, their emotions were being sidetracked and expressed reactively. The sad and tender emotions aren't "cool" for adolescent males to express, so they have to be covered up.

Medical research has documented a greater rate of stress-related illnesses among males. At all age levels, males more than females are likely to suffer from ulcers, high blood pressure and heart attacks. Other research has confirmed the toll the traditional male role has upon psychological health. Males who disclose themselves less to others are more likely to have psychological problems, including neurotic symptoms, poorer interpersonal functioning and effectiveness and poorer personal adjustment. Research has also found that men with traditional sex-role orientation reported lower levels of health and life satisfaction.

The costs to male friendships. Another result of traditional roles is that men's relationships with other men are often superficial. In his study on male intimacy, Michael McGill (1985:184) reports that even the best of friends "reveal so little of themselves to each other that they are little more than acquaintances. There is no intimacy in most male relationships and none of what intimacy offers: solace and support."

Men are less able than women to relate in an open, vulnerable way to the same sex. As we shall see in chapters six and twelve, two traditional male characteristics seem to account for this: homophobia and competition.

Homophobia is the fear of being close to a person of the same sex. American males tend to be fearful of being branded as homosexual or of having homosexual tendencies. But the more secure men are in their sexuality, the more open they can be in relating to one another. Men who are secure in their own masculinity can greet one another with a hug, show sympathy by gently putting an arm around the shoulder of another, and verbally express affection to each other.

Although most men would probably deny that they are "skin-hungry," they often need to be physically stroked and held. In recounting their favorite growing-up memories, brothers will often talk about how they playfully wrestled with each other. Perhaps their need for physical closeness was met through an acceptably masculine way of touching.

In many cultures around the world, men openly express their friendship by kissing each other on one cheek and then the other. In the Near and Far East, male friends may converse with their arms around each other. Compared to most other cultures of the world, the American culture pressures men to be decidedly inhibited about showing love and affection to another man.

Competition can also be a barrier to open, vulnerable relationships between males. In the business world, men often compete fiercely for status based on the number of sales they make, the salary they earn or the placement of their office relative to the president's. Such competition works against business productivity and close personal relationships when men withhold information out of fear that someone else will use it to outperform them.

In his book *Male Chauvinism: How It Works*, Michael Korda tells how illicit sex becomes a status symbol in the corporate world. Men may brag to each other about the number of sexual conquests they have achieved among the women in the office.

When there are no traditional status symbols that can be used to determine rank, men will invent them. In prison, for example, where all symbols of status are stripped away, an inmate may establish status by being the best at playing cards or eating the most food.

Recent research suggests that men do not become more intimate with each other because of the organization structures they work in. One study, for example, found that delivery men in a cookie company who held similar jobs with low supervision, high security and a noncompetitive environment developed intimate friendship ties and met frequently off the job. A comparison group of people who worked in a highly differentiated, competitive factory related to one another only as associates and had infrequent outside contact. So it seems that if men are exposed long enough to social structures that are noncompetitive and not achievement-oriented, male intimacy has a greater chance to develop.

The cost to our marriages. Wives' most common complaint about their husbands is that there is little intimacy between them. Generally, women desire more intimacy and men desire more sex. The traditional male has difficulty bringing the two together. After several years, many wives give up on the struggle for intimacy, surrendering to the view that "men are just that way!"

The most serious by-product of the traditional sex roles is domestic violence. One study reported that men who held more traditional opinions about sex roles were more likely to endorse the use of physical force in marriage. Another found that violent husbands were significantly less assertive than men in satisfactory, nonviolent relationships. In a study of men who had physically abused their wives, it was found that these men believed that they must be strong, dominant, superior and successful; but they themselves felt devastated and inadequate (Coleman 1980). In reaction to being dependent upon their wives, they tended to distance themselves by complaining about their wives' ineffectiveness as mothers and housekeepers. The physical abuse was an attempt to cover up the inadequacy these men felt in relation to their wives.

The cost to children. As a result of the work patterns that developed out of the Industrial Revolution, fathers have come to spend less and less time with their children. In families where the father worked outside the home and the mother worked within the home, most parenting became mothering. The cost to children has been a lack of closeness with their fathers.

In his 1986 study, Samuel Osherson found that many men describe their fathers as rejecting, absent and incompetent as fathers. He suggested that men have a "wounded father within," an image of a father who was not there for them, not available when they needed attention or advice from a dad. Both males and females describe their relationship with their mothers in more intimate and caring terms than their relationship with their fathers. More than anything else, most children today need stronger fathering—and this, as we shall see in chapter eleven, will greatly benefit mothers and fathers as well.

The cost to women. Recently there's been an avalanche of books on how traditional male roles have hurt women. In the widely read *Women Who Love Too Much* (1985), Robin Norwood describes the dilemma facing women who have invested themselves in a relationship with a man, only to find they are receiving very little emotional support in return. It is significant that the subtitle to Norwood's book is *When You Keep Wishing and Hoping He'll Change.* Norwood believes that many women whose husbands cannot fully love back labor under the illusion that if they will just love a little bit more, then surely their husbands will reciprocate. Unfortunately, according to Norwood, there's little evidence that men can be expected to change.

Susan Forward and Joan Torres's book *Men Who Hate Women and the Women Who Love Them* (1986) was another national best-seller that dealt with emotional imbalance in female-male relationships. The authors believe many women are caught up in relationships with men who cause them tremendous pain. Such men intimidate by yelling or withdrawing into angry silence; switch from charm to anger without warning; belittle women's opinions, feelings and accomplishments; withdraw love, money, approval or sex as a form of punishment or control; or humiliate their wives in front of others. An ad targeted to women readers says, "Alone, he may not be able to help himself control his behavior. But *you can*. Because, of course, this is *not* the way love is supposed to feel. And understanding your man's destructive pattern, and the part you play in it, is the first step in breaking the pattern, healing the hurt, and regaining vital self-respect and confidence."

Men at the Crossroads

These are hard times for men. American society is short-changing males. We are being encouraged to discard the male script that was given to us at birth and has been our guide through life. As we grew up, society taught us that to be a male was to be strong, tough, rational and inexpressive of our feelings, but we're now being told that this model is obsolete. We're experiencing a "discontinuity in cultural conditioning" which the anthropologist Ruth Benedict (1938) spoke of more than fifty years ago.

Yet this difficult time can also be a time of enormous opportunity—for personal growth and greater closeness with those we love most. Men are, in fact, at a crossroads. One road offers the known security of being a traditional male. In the opposite direction is the pull to become a "modern" man and pursue some androgynous ideal. But closer examination reveals that these aren't the only two options. There are a variety of other paths branching out of our crossroads.

In the next two chapters we'll consider several of these roads in more detail. We will then be in a position to consider a radical alternative— a Christian model of manhood.

PART II

In Search of the Real Man

2
WHY ARE MEN DIFFERENT FROM WOMEN?
The Traditional Male and the Feminist Challenge

Generally, men still are best at the cognitive, rational mode that work requires, so it's where they turn for validation. Usually, women still are more comfortable in the emotional and experimental mode that interpersonal connections require, so that's where they look for fulfillment. For men, therefore, it's still work that gets their first allegiance, if not in word, then in deed; for women it's still love.

LILLIAN RUBIN, *INTIMATE STRANGERS*

Denise, Erin and Gloria, seniors in college, are having a late-Saturday-night discussion in a dorm room. The topic, *men,* is not an uncommon one, since all three are dating with some regularity. Denise, who has been in a steady relationship with Tom for eight months, opens the topic by confiding her wish that Tom were more able to communicate on the feeling level. Seizing the opportunity to apply insights she is learning in her course on "Culture and Feminism," Erin replies, "Withholding their feelings is merely a ploy men use to maintain power in relationships with women."

Gloria objects, "No, I think men are less able to operate on the feeling level because they are born that way. My boyfriend, Jim, is a biology major, and he explained to me that this is a result of a natural selection process. Nurturant females and strong, protective males were more successful in passing . . ."

But before she can finish, Erin retorts, "That's a perfect example of the intellectual rationalizations men develop to justify their more powerful position in society. Any man I date will not get away with such bull!"

Denise counters, "I think you are both wrong. I find Tom wants to express his feelings, but has difficulty doing so because in growing up he was taught that it's unmanly to be emotional."

Needless to say, men who encounter Denise, Erin and Gloria will experience completely different perspectives regarding men. Because these differences are based upon alternative explanations of gender difference, and because these various explanations affect men's attitudes about themselves, it's essential that we develop a good understanding of them. After exploring these interpretations of gender differences, I will summarize the case that has been made for the traditional male, as well as the challenge to this model from radical feminists and the early men's movement.

Why Are Men and Women Different?

Explanations for gender differences have taken different positions on the nurture-versus-nature argument. This controversy coincided with the emergence of modern science. With the development of the biological sciences, it was discovered that genetics played a key role in determining many aspects of life. Both physical features and temperamental traits were seen as resulting from genetic packages that children inherited from their parents. Although each individual's genetic package was understood to be different, males and females in general were also thought to possess decidedly different packages.

Social scientists challenged this notion by arguing that existing gender differences were acquired after birth through cultural conditioning. Those arguing on either side initially assumed an either-or approach: gender differences must be either a result of hereditary factors or a result of environmental factors—not a combination of the two.

As the dividing lines between scientific disciplines have broken down, explanations for gender differences have become less of an "all-or-nothing" proposition. Contemporary explanations of gender differences are now much more complex, and both behavioral and biological scientists point to an interactive effect of heredity and environment.

The women's movement of the 1970s brought heightened attempts to explain the origins of gender differences. The theories of that decade tended to emphasize the role of nurture (environment).

Social-Environmental Explanations
Socialization theory. According to socialization theory, from the time children are born they are taught explicitly and implicitly how to be a man or how to be a woman. The boy in American society comes to value masculinity as expressed through physical courage, toughness, competitiveness, strength, control, courage, dominance and aggressiveness. It's argued that the American girl begins to value femininity as expressed through gentleness, expressiveness, responsiveness, sensitivity and compliance.

When parents harshly enforce these distinctions in early childhood, boys learn to fear and avoid being caught doing anything that is traditionally defined as feminine. Girls will avoid appearing too aggressive, boisterous or "tomboyish" for fear of being branded "unladylike."

As children move away from the sphere of family influence, their peer groups continue to perpetuate these gender-role stereotypes. According to studies of male subcultures such as school groups and street-corner gangs, if a male is affectionate, gentle or compassionate he is not invited to be "one of the boys." Girls are ostracized in a similar way. The mass media reinforces these same traditional stereotypes subtly yet powerfully through comics, magazine advertisements, TV programs and the movies.

The message of how to be female and male is deeply imprinted in the cultural patterns of every society. In North America, the family, peer group and mass media converge to persuade young females and males to take on stereotypical gender behaviors. By the time males and females reach adulthood, they have been socialized into clearly defined, sexually determined roles.

Feminist theories. The feminist theories also explain gender differences in terms of social-environmental factors. The majority wing of the feminist movement consists of *liberal feminists* who use socialization theory to explain gender differences. They point to inequality of opportunity within the social structure—a system in which men are the dominant class and women are the underclass. Although not all liberal feminists deny the possibility of some innate differences between the sexes, they believe that most of the difference is socially determined. They believe that persons, irrespective of sex, have individual skills and abilities.

Advocates of *Marxist feminism* believe that gender equality is possible only in a classless society. In their view, class differences and private property cyclically perpetuate the oppression of women. *Radical feminists* argue that the oppression of women is fundamental in the nature of male-female relationships—that it existed before the emergence of private property. Contrary to Marxist feminists, radical feminists do not believe that setting up a "classless" society will end the oppression of women. Rather, sexism is understood to be rooted in the very fabric of all societies and will not diminish, apart from intentional and structural change. *Socialist feminists* accept the major arguments of both Marxist and radical feminism; they argue that *both* economic and sexual oppression are primary causes of sexism.

Sociobiology
Not content to explain the social behavior of insects and animals, biologists have recently invaded the territory traditionally staked out by the social scientists. The biologically based explanation of humans' social behavior is known as sociobiology. Sociobiology seeks to explain male aggression in terms of innate genetic makeup.

Needless to say, this has resulted in a sharp debate within the social sciences. Some argue that sociobiology is actually as nonempirical as any religion, and so requires a return to prescientific metaphysics. Others predict that sociobiology will provide such valuable explanations that sociology will become obsolete.

The sociobiological explanation usually starts with a description of the need for gender-based economic role divisions among our early ancestors. In one version (Tiger 1969; Tiger and Fox 1971), men developed a sense of adventurous protectiveness toward their family because of the need to bond together in hunting wild animals. This is known as the bonding instinct. Women, on the other hand, developed nurturing abilities because of their need to bear and rear children.

One may ask, what prevented women from going with the men on the hunt? Lionel Tiger's research indicates that some women did hunt, but it lessened the chances that their offspring would survive. This minimized the evolution of the gene pool from generation to generation. Additionally, women who spent their time safely at home giving birth to and caring for children were desired more as marriage partners. Consequently, these were the women who succeeded in passing on their genes to future generations.

The men who were desired as marriage partners were not those who stayed in the compound caring for children, but those who were successful in the hunt. Thus, it was not the men with nurturing tendencies who successfully contributed to the ongoing gene pool, but those who acted on their bonding instinct.

The inferred result is that men and women have different genetic packages. While women are perceived as more capable of emotional bonding with small children, men are identified as being more adventurous, strong and protective of their families.

Sociobiology explains temperamental differences between the genders as a reflection of differences in genetic packages. Sociobiologists may agree that since we no longer live in a society dependent upon hunting dangerous animals, the differences between the sexes are no longer functional. But they do argue that these genetically produced differences are real and cannot simply be dismissed.

Christians differ in how they view sociobiology. Some reject any speculation about the origin of gender differences, and others believe that temperamental differences are part of God's creation of male and female nature. The dialog continues today.

A Nature-Nurture Synthesis

Figure 1 lays out the logical alternative explanations of gender differences. The arrow leading from "Nurture" to "Gender Differences" represents a *social determinist* position, which explains gender differences solely on the basis of sociocultural factors. There are several kinds of social determinism. *Biological determinism* explains gender difference in purely natural (genetic and physiological) terms. *Theistic determinism* holds that gender differences are innate and created by God. In chapter four I will present evidence that gender differences may be a result of the curse placed upon women and men after the Fall. The arrows leading from "God" to "Nurture" and "Nature" represent the position that God can work through nurture *or* nature to bring about desirable gender differences.

Figure 1. Explanations of Gender Differences

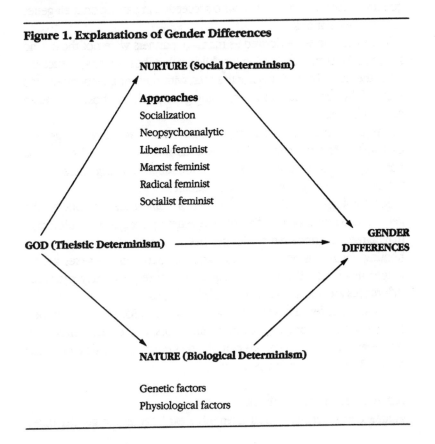

Personally, I reject both social and biological determinism, though I accept the evidence that both nature and nurture contribute to gender differences. Reviewing all the evidence pertaining to gender differences, Alice Rossi (1984:11) concluded that "organisms are not passive objects acted upon by internal genetic forces, as some sociobiologists claim, nor are they passive objects acted upon by external environmental forces, as some social scientists claim. . . [G]enes, organisms, and environment interpenetrate and mutually determine each other." Drawing from five areas of research, Rossi finds compelling evidence that biological factors account for some gender differences. The five areas include (1) correlations between social behavior and physiological sex attributes; (2) gender differences in infants and young children before they have experienced much socialization; (3) the emergence of gender differences in puberty, when physiology and hormonal secretion change rapidly; (4) gender differences that are stable across cultures; and (5) similar gender differences among species of higher primates.

Rossi also cites evidence indicating that women have a "head start" in caring for children in their earliest years, when they are learning language. Female infants show higher sensitivity to touch, sound and odor; they are more attracted to human faces and more responsive to the nuances of facial expression. In addition, girls learn to talk more quickly, have greater memory retention, are more sensitive to context, develop greater skill in picking up peripheral information and process information more quickly. Rossi believes that all these advantages make it easier for females to make the connection between feelings and their expression in words.

Though these findings may seem to reinforce traditional gender stereotypes, they do not rule out the possibility that these tendencies are *accentuated* through socialization. On the basis of both social-science and physiological research, we can say that males and females are born with *general dispositions,* but not *directional predispositions.* This means that though research on infants shows that females have a head start at expressing their feelings, we should see males as merely "behind"; we need not fatalistically expect males to be unable to express their feelings at all.

What usually happens is that genetic tendencies are exaggerated by patterns of socialization to fit in with the prevailing definition of masculinity and femininity. (See figure 2, where the distance between the horizontal lines represents the difference between male and female behavior.) I'd suggest that it's culture, not biology, that molds males to appear *primarily* dominant and rational and shapes females to appear submissive and emotional. Although natural tendencies are often magnified by nurture, nurture could just as well diminish these differences between males and females.

I reject a theistic determinism that argues that God has placed a full-blown masculine imprint on men and a full-blown feminine imprint on women. Rather, gender identity is a reflection of both sociocultural *and* biological factors. If this is so, we can expect as much variety *among* males and females as *between* the two sexes. Still, the evidence shows that there will be general or average differences between males and females.

This is what I've tried to represent in figure 1. The small differences produced by biology are made large by culture. At the left side of figure 1, I suggest that biblical evidence for gender differences corresponds more closely to biological gender difference than to culturally produced differences. I will discuss this point again in chapter four.

The Case for the Traditional Male

Who is the traditional male? The question is both easy and difficult to answer. It's easy because most of us men have been socialized to be traditional males. Yet traditional masculinity is difficult to understand for the same reason: it's so much a part of who we are. We're like fish that can't understand "water" until they are flopping about in a fishing net. We can best understand traditional masculinity by removing ourselves from the cultural encasement within which the traditional male exists.

Men have traditionally been defined as independent, oriented toward tasks and achievement, objective, competitive, rational, unsentimental, dominant, aggressive, sexually active and inexpressive, while women have been defined as dependent, interpersonally oriented, sentimental, emotionally supportive, submissive, nurturing, sexually inactive and expressive. Debra David and Robert Brannon (1976) have identified four major themes in the traditional male role.

The first theme is *The Big Wheel,* which has to do with how we define success. Traditionally, women have felt good about themselves when they were successful in interpersonal relationships—as a wife, mother, friend and so on. Men, on the other hand, felt good about themselves only by achieving in some objective way. An educational degree, a good job, a promotion, a high salary or a prestigious honor allowed a man to feel good about himself. Men whose self-worth is based on achievement will drive themselves in order to obtain the symbols of that success.

A related theme is *The Sturdy Oak,* which refers to the expectation that men need to be strong, tough, confident and self-reliant. Men must especially be strong in crisis or hardship. The cliché "When things get tough, the tough get going" applies here. The real man can face danger and even death in the eye and not blink. The implication is that men need to be strong for others, such as women and children, because these others may not be able to be strong for themselves. Like sturdy oaks, men can be relied upon for strength and endurance.

The third theme is *Give 'Em Hell!*—the expectation that men are daring, adventuresome, aggressive and even violent. Men's cries at sports events reveal that the traditional male's ambition for his team goes beyond the desire to win. "Kill him!" "Break his arm off!" "Smash the sucker!"

Yet manhood includes not only what men *should* do, but also what a real man should *not* do—thus the final theme, *No Sissy Stuff.* This theme gives a *negative* definition to masculinity. A good portion of this theme involves men avoiding being—or even giving the appearance of being—feminine. Generally, boys spend most of their growing-up years under the nurture, supervision and guidance of their mother and female schoolteachers. If a male is much closer to his mother than to his father, he will likely tend to define his manhood by negating femininity. Another important portion of the "no-sissy-stuff" theme is many men's difficulty in expressing their feelings. In chapter five we'll consider how male inexpressiveness creates a barrier to intimacy.

One of the best attempts to defend the traditional male role was given by Brigitte and Peter Berger in their book *The War over the Family* (1983). The Bergers admit that what we call "traditional" gender roles in reality evolved over the past two hundred years in response to industrialization. With industrialization came a new middle-class type of family that was different from aristocratic families. In this new family, the public sphere of work was separated from the private sphere of the home. Before industrialization, home and work life had been intertwined, with both husbands and wives participating in each.

The middle-class family developed a division of labor according to gender. The home became women's domain. "Within the household, the woman is the 'homemaker'-companion and helper to her husband, supervisor and 'facilitator' of her children's development and education, arbiter of taste, culture, and all the 'finer things of life' " (Berger and Berger 1983:102). Work in the marketplace became the men's domain. In this new family, girls were socialized to be homemakers as they learned to cook, sew, take care of children and manage a household. Boys were prepared to take on wage-earning jobs outside the home.

The Bergers essentially present a *functional* argument for a division of labor in which mothers take care of the children and fathers earn a living outside the home. Children need the stability and love of a full-time parent. Citing anthropological evidence, the Bergers conclude that it isn't essential for both parents to have the same intensive interaction with their children; but a "mother figure" (the mother or another woman) is definitely needed. They admit that it may be *theoretically* possible for a male to play the role of a "mother figure." But, they conclude, if such an arrangement can produce healthy infants, why has it not been successfully tried somewhere?

The gender-based division of labor worked to produce the male and female personalities that the new system needed. Boys grew up being rational, emotionally closed and aggressive because they needed these qualities if they were to survive in the marketplace. Girls grew up being sensitive, nurturing and expressive of their feelings because caretakers of children would need these qualities. So, according to the Bergers, much of the difference between males and females is a *functional* adaptation to the structural needs of industrial society. On this basis the

Bergers defend traditional gender roles:

> We believe that there is no viable alternative to the bourgeois family for the raising of children who will have a good chance of becoming responsible and autonomous individuals, nor do we see alternative arrangements by which adults, from youth to old age, will be given a stable context for the affirmation of themselves and their values. The defense of the bourgeois family, therefore, is not an exercise in romantic nostalgia. It is something to be undertaken in defense of human happiness and human dignity in a difficult time. (Berger and Berger 1983:167)

"Christian" defenses of traditional gender roles sometimes borrow from such functionalist reasoning. They go on to argue that God has ordained that men work outside the home, while women stay at home with their children. For married women to work outside the home, especially while their children are young, is viewed as a violation of God's design. Many Christians who defend traditional gender roles do not realize that they are defending a system that has existed only since the Industrial Revolution—a fairly recent event in human history.

Having considered the case for "traditional" roles, let's examine the principal challenges to those roles.

The Feminist Challenge

Besides sharing the fervent hope of eliminating sexism, most feminist theories identify gender differences as resulting from sociocultural factors. Specifically, patriarchy is thought to have been a central obstacle to the affirmation of women as persons throughout history. Feminists feel the frustration of this obstruction and say we need to change the social and institutional structures that perpetuate women's subordinate status. The traditional male role is seen as part and parcel of a repressive patriarchal system.

Most feminists are in favor of doing away with gender-based social roles. Assuming the sexes' equal potential, liberal feminists believe that gender should not determine involvement in any family or societal task. All individuals should be allowed to pursue their own goals, respective of gender, and participate in any task or activity they choose.

But liberal feminists also argue for a variety of family forms as a constructive and healthy response to modern society. The complexity of modern life, they say, calls for different family arrangements in which individuals of both sexes have a free choice in their wage-earning and home-keeping roles. The male wage-earner/housewife configuration is one possibility; other options include female wage-earner/househusband and dual-earners/dual-housekeeping forms. Liberal feminists call for tolerance: allowing and encouraging people to develop the type of living arrangement that is best for them. They abhor the bondage and constriction of rigidly defined female and male roles.

Radical feminists go a step further and seek the elimination of male and female differences. They argue that radical change is needed in three areas. First, they believe that economic freedom can develop only as women form their own economic associations and businesses. Our society, they say, is currently geared to reward the male rather than the female; thus women are generally in economic bondage to men. Women's progress to date is seen as mere tokenism, involving only a few females who have been given highly visible positions in the economic and political structure. Capitalist organizations, controlled by men, freeze the economic subordination of women through the male-oriented subculture. Liberal and radical feminists alike pointed to the glaring absence of women at the 1991 Senate hearing on the confirmation of Supreme Court Justice Clarence Thomas. The hearing committee consisted entirely of white males, who were to judge the competence of a black male judge and the credibility of a black female's claims that he sexually harassed her.

Second, radicals argue that women must be allowed sexual freedom—to establish spontaneous sexual relationships with anyone they choose. This means putting an end to the hypocritical double standard which gives much more sexual freedom to men. In the minds of radical feminists, it also means the freedom to choose same-sex relationships.

Third, radical feminists believe women need to be freed from the burden of rearing and caring for children. This task should be shared not only by fathers but also by society as a whole. Women will be truly liberated, then, once they are freed from the demanding and time-consuming tasks of child care.

Radical feminism tends to reject masculine and feminine distinctives in favor of talking about *human* distinctives. They believe personal distinctiveness should be based on one's choices, not on gender-related categories. Radical feminism views traditional masculinity as an attempt to perpetuate gender-based distinctives.

The Challenge of the Early Men's Movement

There are two separate strands to the modern men's movement, each developing quite independently of the other. The early men's movement dates back to the early 1970s. As the women's movement gained momentum, men who were supportive of women's goals searched for ways to act out their support. It wasn't easy for men to participate directly in the women's movement. To keep from diluting their political goals, many women believed that they needed a movement *for* women *by* women. We men who were sympathetic to women's goals received a loud, clear message: WHY DON'T YOU TRY TO DO SOMETHING ABOUT THE SEXISM IN *MEN?*

If the problem women were experiencing was sexism, then men were in fact the people most in need of change. So the men's movement began as a consciousness-raising experience.

Just as the women's movement sought to help women see how they were being discriminated against, the men's movement focused on raising men's consciousness of how they were individually and collectively responsible for repressing women. To be involved in the early men's movement was to support the women's movement.

But as we began to deal with our own issues, we quickly found that we men were also held captive by the traditionally defined male role. We came to realize that the same traditional male values that had led to the oppression of women had also crippled *us* badly. We discovered that there was a personal cost to our quest to dominate and be in control.

Having experienced the pressure to compete with others and to "win at all costs," we sought the virtue of cooperating with other men. In response to an emphasis on appearing strong and hard, we sought the virtue of softness and openness. In response to an emphasis on independence and self-sufficiency, we sought the virtue of vulnerability and neediness. No longer putting down "sissy" or "feminine" behavior, we sought the virtues of nurture, expressiveness and caring.

Our goal was to create a new male, one that was more feminine than the macho one we had been raised to emulate. Notice this theme in a chapter title of Herb Goldberg's 1979 book *The New Male*—"The Feminist Movement Can Save Your Life." The movement increasingly developed not only a profeminine emphasis but also an *antimasculine* attitude. This attitude is expressed in another of Goldberg's chapter titles: "Self-Destruction Is Masculine, Getting Better Is Feminine."

The leaders of the early men's movement had been heavily influenced by socialization theory. The underlying assumption was that males (and females) are born with a clean slate upon which society "imprints" its definition of masculinity. This view is best illustrated in the writings of Joseph Pleck, who has legitimately been called the father of men's studies (Brod 1987; Franklin 1988). In his important book *The Myth of Masculinity,* Pleck rejects the notion that individuals have "preprogrammed . . . innate psychological needs" to develop a sex-role identity. The central determinants of sex-typed traits, then, are sociocultural factors such as *social approval* and *situational adaptation* rather than innate psychological needs.

In theoretical jargon, leaders in the early men's (as well as women's) movement were *structuralists.* A structuralist sees masculinity (and femininity) as a purely social construct. The emergence of personal characteristics is explained in terms of the structures within which individuals are socialized.[1] Implicit in this explanation is an assumption regarding how gender roles are best changed: before undesirable sexist characteristics can be reduced or eliminated, the social structures that bring about these characteristics must be changed.

The men's movement grew slowly during the 1970s and did not get

---

[1]There are many types of structuralists. A Marxist feminist, for example, explains sexism in terms of capitalist economic structures, while a radical feminist refers to patriarchy. But in both cases, the social structure is used to explain any difference in character traits between women and men.

organized on the national level until 1983, with the emergence of the National Organization for Changing Men (NOCM). Although the NOCM met annually and had a number of regional chapters and a regular newsletter called *Brother*, it failed to capture the attention of the large majority of American males.

The effectiveness of the men's movement has been limited by two nagging issues—sexual preference and race. Even at the 1974 men's conference I attended, there was considerable discussion on the relationship between gay and straight men in the movement. The fact that NOCM's Statement of Principles takes a pro-gay stance has undoubtedly discouraged some straights from participating in it. Meanwhile, blacks within the movement question whether its participants are giving enough attention to the problem of racism toward the black male. They argue that racism is a men's issue because "white males have been the greatest perpetrators of and reaped the most benefits from racism throughout history" (Franklin 1988:19).

The early men's movement was most effective in reaching men in academic circles. It was influential in the establishment of men's studies programs on several campuses, and in convincing directors of some existing women's studies programs to expand to women's *and* men's studies. It played a vital role in supporting the legitimate concerns of feminists and in helping men to become aware of their own imprisonment in roles.

As members of the movement challenged traditional masculinity, however, they unfortunately failed to see the strengths and positive qualities in the traditional male. Rejecting the traditional male's excessive emphasis upon strength, the early men's movement too often led to, as we shall see in the next chapter, what Robert Bly refers to as "the soft male."

3

THE NEW MALE
King, Warrior, Magician and Lover

Our obligation—and I include in "our" all the women and men writing about gender—is to describe *masculine* in such a way that it does not exclude the masculine in women, and yet hits a resonant string in the man's heart too— but in the man's heart there is a low string that makes his whole chest tremble when the qualities of the masculine are spoken of in the right way.

ROBERT BLY, *IRON JOHN*

Although the new men's movement began to stir in the early 1980s, it wasn't until the broadcast of Bill Moyers' PBS interview with Robert Bly, "A Gathering of Men," in 1989 that the movement burst as water released from a floodgate upon the American scene. With the publication of Robert Bly's book *Iron John* in 1990, for the first time in history a book about men made it to the top-ten nonfiction bestseller list—and it stayed there for thirty weeks. In 1991 Sam Keen's book *Fire in My Belly* likewise rose to the top-ten list.

It needs to be emphasized that the new men's movement is not a direct outgrowth of the early movement I described in chapter two. *The Making of Masculinities: The New Men's Studies,* a 1988 collection of pieces by the acknowledged leaders of the early men's movement, included not one reference in its 346 pages to Joseph Campbell, Robert Bly, Robert Moore or Douglas Gillette, the most influential thinkers and spokesmen of the new men's movement. Nor do Robert Bly in *Iron John* and Robert Moore and Douglas Gillette in *King, Warrior, Magician, Lover* feel the need to cite the writings of persons in the early men's movement.

Why has the new men's movement received greater publicity? Is it merely a matter of timing? Were the majority of men not prepared in the 1970s and 1980s to deal with men's issues, as they seem to be in the 1990s? Did the full message of the women's movement need to sink in before men were able to examine themselves as males? A yes to each of these questions carries some truth. But there are also some significant differences between the early and new men's movements.

First, and probably most important, the new men's movement rejects the cultural determinist position of the early movement. The subtitle of Moore and Gillette's book is *Rediscovering the Archetypes of the Mature Masculine*. Rather than assuming that masculinity is a purely social construct, the leaders in the new movement assume that there are "fundamental deep structures of the human self, both masculine and feminine" (Moore and Gillette 1990:xi).

Second, the new men's movement seeks to affirm a full range of masculinity, rather than merely calling men to develop their "feminine" side. Bly (1990:3) forcefully states this in an observation he makes about men affected by the early men's movement:

In the seventies I began to see all over the country a phenomenon that we might call the "soft male." Sometimes even today when I look out at an audience, perhaps half the young males are what I'd call soft. They're lovely, valuable people—I like them—they're not interested in harming the earth or starting wars. There's a gentle attitude toward life in their whole being and style of living. But many of these men are not happy. You quickly notice the lack of energy in them. They are life-preserving but not exactly life-giving. Ironically, you often see these men with strong women who positively radiate energy. Here we have a finely turned young man, ecologically superior to his father, sympathetic to the whole harmony of the universe, yet he himself has little vitality to offer.

Bly (1990:4) concludes his evaluation of the early men's movement as follows: "The journey many American men have taken into softness, or receptivity, or 'development of the feminine side,' has been an immensely valuable journey, but more travel lies ahead." We turn now to what the new men's movement offers for men's journey into full manhood.

The Problem

According to the new men's movement, men suffer because they have been hindered from developing into the men they could be. Male development has been retarded due to the absence of strong male role models, a result of the Industrial Revolution. In fact, the Industrial Revolution did much more harm to sons than to daughters, because by removing the father from the home it kept sons from learning the male mode of thinking and feeling.

Bly suggests that when the typical father returns home after working all day, he is too tired and drained to be the male role model his son needs. The father cannot take time to answer his son's many questions, explain to him how things work and help him learn to be a man by doing things with him. Also, the typical father is convinced that he is an inadequate human being because he hears this message constantly. For example, wives want from their husbands what they didn't get from their fathers, but find their husbands can't meet the need because they weren't fathered either.

We are a society without a father, and a nation of men who have a hole in their psyches because their fathers were not there. Bly cites the German writer Alexander Mitscherlich to suggest that the hole in a son's psyche can be filled only by demons. "When the son does not see his father's work place, or what he produces, does he imagine his father to be a hero, a fighter for good, a saint, or a white knight? Alexander Mitscherlich's answer is sad: demons move into that empty place." Is it any wonder, Bly asks, that during the 1960s, after the older men betrayed the younger men by sending them to be killed in a meaningless war, that young people declared, "Never trust anyone over thirty"? As added evidence, consider the destructive behavior of urban gangs—which are composed almost entirely of boys reared without fathers.

Men today not only have been deprived of a bonded relationship with a strong father, but they have also had inadequate mentoring from adult males. As Bly explains it, in nonindustrial societies men take boys away from their mothers at puberty. Although the mothers ritually protest the loss of their boys, they know they must lose their sons in order for them to become men. The adult men of the village initiate the boys into manhood by forcing them to go through puberty rites. Only adult men are capable of doing the initiating.

Where are mentors and initiators of men in modern society? For most young men there are none. The tragic drama being played out in the urban gang is that boys are trying to initiate boys. Such gangs inevitably develop destructive codes of masculinity—proving one's toughness by destroying others or other people's property.

The Answer: Masculine Archetypes

Part of the appeal of the new men's movement is that it offers men a masculine ideal rather than a fuzzy, culturally relative notion. Its masculine ideal is based upon the existential psychology of Carl Jung. Jungian psychology suggests that within every man there is a feminine subpersonality, just as within every woman there is a masculine subpersonality. Every man needs to get in touch with his feminine side—but without rejecting his masculine personality.

There are four archetypes within the masculine personality—the *king*, the *warrior*, the *magician* and the *lover* (see Moore and Gillette 1990). These archetypes reside on the deep unconscious level of the psyche. They are grounded in what Jung called the "collective unconscious," which is made up of instinctual patterns and energy configurations probably inherited genetically throughout the generations of our species. Jungians believe that these archetypes are the foundations of our behavior, thinking and emotions (Moore and Gillette 1990:9).

Two forms of evidence are offered in support of these archetypes. The first form consists of "mountains of clinical evidence" accumulated from psychological analysis of patients' dreams and daydreams, as well as from careful observations of human behavior. The second kind of evidence is in-depth studies of mythology and folklore around the world (Moore and Gillette 1990:10).

Represented in table 1 are the four masculine archetypes, along with the passive and active deficiencies of each. Since these concepts are extremely important in the new men's movement, I will give a detailed description of each archetype before offering a critique of the new male.

Table 1. Ideal and Deficient Masculine Archetypes

Passive Deficient	Ideal	Active Deficient
Weakling	King	Tyrant
Masochist	Warrior	Sadist
Denying "Innocent" One	Magician	Detached Manipulator
Impotent Lover	Lover	Addicted Lover

The King. Within every male there is a king. The good king is the image of God within every man, known for his good judgment, wisdom and selflessness. A healthy king's energy is regenerative as he performs two functions. First, the king *orders* reality, as represented in the self, by maintaining the balance between the warrior, the magician and the lover. The king only secondarily reinforces order, since he primarily models order by living the order in his own life.

Second, the king's energy provides *fertility* and *blessing.* The healthy king has the energy to engage in sexual acts that produce children, and his energy also helps the material aspects of the kingdom—land, cattle, crops and commerce—to flourish. The king provides blessing by affirming others who deserve it. The good king delights in his subjects by rewarding them and bestowing honor upon them for their good service.

The good king possesses the qualities of ordering, of rational and reasonable patterning, of integrity and integration in the masculine psyche. This archetype provides psychic stability and centeredness, maintaining balance where otherwise there might be emotional chaos and out-of-control behaviors.

But not all kings in the male psyche are good and strong. When the king is too aggressive he becomes the *tyrant*; when he is too passive he is the *weakling.* Like the king who had his younger brothers killed so they could not compete for his throne, the tyrant within the male psyche is jealous of younger males and seeks to demasculinize them. Mercilessly and without feeling, the tyrant abuses and exploits others. To win is not enough; the perceived enemy must be degraded and humiliated. The tyrant will especially lash out against those who possess the very inner qualities and strengths he lacks. Men who verbally or physically abuse their wives or children have given in to a tyrant who is but a shadow king. The tyrant may appear strong, but on the inside—within the psyche—he is weak, fearful and impotent. When threatened, the tyrant may show rage, but inside he is weak and easily deflated.

You see how easily the tyrant flip-flops to his polar opposite, the weakling. The weakling lacks security, calmness and centeredness. If he can't control a truly strong person through threats and intimidation, he will avoid that person. Instead, he will pick on the weak mercilessly—with such force that he seems to be actually attacking the weakness in himself.

Many weaklings in essence abdicate the kingly throne by becoming completely dependent upon a more powerful person. The weakling is especially susceptible to being ruled by a person whose position in the social order allows him to be a tyrant. By attaching themselves to tyrants, weaklings vicariously join in terrorizing others.

The Warrior. Within the men's and women's movements of the 1970s, the warrior became a part of manhood to be repudiated. But the thinkers within the new men's movement believe this was a mistake. Attempting to deny or repress the warrior archetype within men is merely to invite it to resurface in another form—as emotional and physical violence. Rightly understood, the good warrior is a necessary part of every healthy male psyche.

The warrior in his fullness takes an aggressive stance toward life. He moves out from a defensive position and seeks to do something about life's tasks and problems. The action the warrior takes is tempered by sound reason—assessing his own strength and the enemy's and selecting the plan of attack that will be most effective. The warrior endures hours of training to ensure that he is well prepared, both physically and emotionally, for battle. When he acts he is in control of his body and mind, taking decisive action, never wavering.

The warrior's energy shows itself in a "transpersonal commitment," for his loyalty goes beyond a particular person or organization and encompasses a higher cause. Although the warrior sometimes destroys, he does so only when this is necessary to accomplish the higher goal.

When the warrior's energy becomes detached from human relationships, the shadow warrior appears. The shadow warrior is noted for his cruelty, which takes bipolar forms—a *sadist* (active) or a *masochist* (passive). The deficiency in both forms results from a lack of control of body, mind and spirit.

The shadow warrior is out of control when he acts. He either lashes out at everything or everyone in his path or passively invites others to lash out at him. War provides an opportunity for the shadow warrior to play out his viciousness against defenseless men, women and children. The shadow warrior was evident in the My Lai massacre during the Vietnam War. The sadistic shadow warrior was also evident during World War I in the revolting behavior of Turkish soldiers who cut open pregnant women, ripped out their unborn babies and hung them around their necks.

But the shadow warrior can also operate in domestic life. How else can we understand the man who beats and abuses the very ones he is supposed to protect—his wife and children?

Within the shadow warrior is an insecure person who is unsure of his self-worth and masculinity. He is weak, but because he despises the weak, he must hate and despise himself. This sets the stage for the passive side of the shadow warrior, the one who, because of his self-disgust, opens himself up to be despised and abused. Masochist shadow warriors may mercilessly abuse themselves under the guise of sacrificing their lives to save others. The masochist has no boundaries protecting himself against the abuse of others.

Although the shadow warrior takes either an active or a passive form, the polar opposite is usually just below the surface. What prevents the shadow warrior from drawing upon true warrior energy is a lack of commitment to some good beyond his personal gain.

The Magician. The magician archetype has the energy of awareness and insight which enables him to be the knower and master of technology. In psychological terms, the magician is the "observing ego" who, because he is detached from life, has the power to watch it and make adjustments to regulate it. Although the magician doesn't have the power to act, he can provide clarity of thinking for the warrior so that he can act properly. The magician is the thoughtful, reflective introvert side of the extroverted warrior.

The magician is an initiator. He assumes responsibility for the rituals for initiating younger or less mature men into the secrets of life. In our modern technological age, the magician's role has been applied to materialistic concerns more than to spiritual concerns. The magician is like the true guru who has secret wisdom, the one who knows and has the power to give this knowledge and wisdom to others.

While the magician contributes to the development of a full, healthy manhood, the shadow magician retards that development. There are two types of shadow magicians. The active perversion of the magician is the *detached manipulator.* Rather than guiding others, the manipulator directs persons in ways they cannot see. This manipulator can be seen in the lies and propaganda that emanate from politically controlled media. In the hands of manipulators, the media manufacture enemies, exaggerate their strength and solicit the people's money in order to build bombs and weapons of destruction. Although the communist-controlled Soviet Union provided the supreme example of such manipulation, Western democracies were not above manipulative tactics. The manipulator controls by giving information selectively, and he is not above giving false and misleading information. While the magician is a good steward of his wisdom and knowledge, the shadow magician wastes his understanding.

The alternative shadow magician—*the denying innocent one*—pretends that he doesn't have needed knowledge. This passive magician does not actively give false information, but merely withholds information. While the manipulator deals in untruths and false information, the innocent one merely hides needed truth. The innocent one lacks energy and is jealous of those who possess it. Although the passive magician is weak, he is slippery and elusive, nearly impossible to confront head-on. When challenged, he will plead "innocence," reacting with hurt bewilderment in an attempt to make the challenger feel ashamed for even questioning his sincerity.

The Lover. The lover is the archetype of healthy embodiment—of being in the world of sensuous pleasure and in one's own body without shame. Being deeply sensual, the lover is sensitive to the splendor of the physical world. This sensitivity enables the lover not merely to sympathize, but to compassionately *empathize* with others and the world of things around him. Passion, not intellect, is the source of the lover's connection to all inner and outer things. The lover's passion is expressed in the human hunger for sex, food, well-being, reproduction and creative adaptation to life's hardships.

And what of the man who is under the influence of the lover? He wants to touch and be touched, physically and emotionally, by everything. He is aesthetically attuned to his environment and wants to encounter the world of sensual experience in its totality. The lover energy is the source of spirituality, especially the mystical quest for oneness with God and all things. The man in touch with lover energy is sensitive to people, including their joys, sorrows, pain, moods and motivations.

Like the previous shadow forms described, the shadow lover takes one of two polar forms and uses the lover energy to destroy himself and others around him. The active form is the *addicted lover*—devoted to hedonistic self-pleasure, refusing to put any limits on his sensual and sexual experiences. The addicted lover is *lost* in an ocean of the senses and lacks a centeredness. Defenseless before his slightest desire, he is drawn first in one direction and then in another. Such persons live chaotic lives of oversensitivity; they lack the detachment necessary to control the fulfillment of their senses.

The shadow lover's addictions may take the usual forms—sex, eating, drinking, smoking, drugs; or he may become obsessed with painting, learning an exotic foreign language or buying vintage cars. A telltale sign that a man is controlled by the addicted lover is *restlessness.* Although he is always searching for something, he's never satisfied. Life is a desperate quest to find the ultimate experience, the greatest adventure. The addicted lover is caught up in what Reinhold Niebuhr described as the sin of sensuality.

At the opposite pole, the man who is out of touch with the lover in his fullness is possessed by the *impotent lover.* This person experiences life in an unfeeling way—lacking enthusiasm, vividness or aliveness. Boredom, listlessness, alienation and depression are the experiences of men possessed by the impotent lover. Such a man can be sexually impotent; he finds nothing sexually stimulating and is unable to experience an erection. He may be so caught up in the pursuit of his career, with its pressures and demands, that his sexual and sensual sensitivity is dulled.

The Whole Man

Rightly understood, the king, warrior, magician and lover form a complementary whole. The four archetypes work to check and balance one another. A man who is controlled by one archetype to the exclusion of the others will lack wholeness and centeredness. The mature male lives with a strong king, warrior, magician and lover, each complementing the other.

None of the archetypes works well alone. The deficient shadow forms of each are most likely to emerge when there isn't a healthy balance among the four. The magician, for example, needs "the King's concern for generativity and generosity, the Warrior's ability to act decisively and with courage, and the Lover's deep and convinced connection to all things" (Moore and Gillette 1990:118).

I believe that the major imbalance among men today results from a deficient lover. As Moore and Gillette point out, the king, the warrior and the magician harmonize quite well with each other. But without the lover, they lead to an existence that is detached from life. Men today are specialists in detachment; we need to know how to overcome this detachment and become more connected to other people. According to Moore and Gillette, the king, the warrior and the magician "need the Lover to energize them, to humanize them, and to give them their ultimate purpose—love. They need the Lover to keep them from becoming sadistic" (1990:140).

The greed of the 1980s, which led to junk bonds, savings and loan failures and a crisis in the banking industry, can best be understood as a deficiency of the lover in the lives of powerful men. How else can we understand the fact that men who already had millions of dollars were willing to use devious means to obtain more?

There is much that is commendable in this view of manhood. It has an intuitive appeal to me because it fits with what I experience. I might wish for a simpler model of masculinity, but my experience tells me that being a man is far from a simple matter. I find that life calls me to be strong, but not too strong; to be vulnerable, but not too vulnerable; to be emotional, but not so emotional that I lose my rational footing. Being a man is difficult because of all the seemingly contradictory requirements life places upon us. By seeing myself as including a king, a warrior, a magician and a lover, I allow myself to move closer to the multidimensional person God created me to be.

An interesting question to ponder would be, What man in history most exemplified an integrated whole consisting of a mature king, warrior, magician and lover? The one whom the writer of Hebrews identified as prophet, priest and king will be nominated in the following chapter as our best model for a Christian view of manhood.

4
THE CHRISTIAN MALE
A Radical Alternative

Perhaps it is no wonder that the women were first at the Cradle and last at the Cross. They had never known a man like this Man—there never had been such another. A prophet and teacher who never nagged at them, never flattered or coaxed or patronised; who never made arch jokes about them, never treated them either as "The women, God help us!" or "The ladies, God bless them!"

DOROTHY SAYERS, *ARE WOMEN HUMAN?*

The present confusion about gender roles has come about because modern society has lost its points of gender anchorage. As Christians we should not despair at the current confusion, but view it as an opportunity to draw upon both Scripture and secular knowledge, with the goal of developing a more Christian model of masculinity than has existed in the past.

In the previous two chapters we've considered several models of manhood. In this chapter I critique the traditional and "new male" models from a Christian perspective. Based upon these critiques, I will suggest that modern men need to consider as a radical alternative—a Christian model of manhood—and I'll present the basis of this model. The remaining ten chapters of the book will fill out some of the details of this model in relation to the major areas of men's lives.

Bases of Authority
Each model of manhood we have considered, by necessity, deals with

the issue of how masculinity is to be distinguished from femininity. We saw in chapter two that a defense of the traditional model of masculinity carries with it a defense of traditional femininity. Just as maleness is defined in terms of strength, toughness, independence and rational coolness, so femininity is defined in terms of softness, vulnerability, dependence and emotionality. Men should be men! They should stop feeling guilty for qualities they do not have. Human completeness comes in the complementarity between men and women. Any attempt to blur the distinction, it is argued, will only weaken both men and women.

In chapter three we considered the men's movement that began in the 1970s as a reaction to the women's movement. Attempting to support women's liberation, these men came to reject traditional masculinity, which they felt was responsible for the oppression of women. In its place came the soft male—one who was sensitive, nurturing, kind and expressive of his feelings. Traditional masculinity was rejected and replaced by traditional femininity, with a dose of assertiveness.

With the emergence of the new men's movement in the 1980s, the traditional male was identified as incomplete, but the "soft male" was also shown to be incomplete. The answer was to put the two male models together. Based on Jungian psychology, which posits both a masculine and a feminine side within each human being, the answer was for males to get in touch with their feminine side while retaining their masculine side. The complete male was multidimensional, possessing the archetypes of a king, a warrior, a magician and a lover.

How can we evaluate each of these models of manhood? Let's begin by examining the *basis of authority* within each model. Supporters of traditional masculinity appeal to the wisdom of history: traditional gender roles have worked in the past, so why tamper with them? Some Christians attempt to infuse Christian morality into the traditional model. Unfortunately, they're not so much interested in *discerning* a biblical perspective on gender roles in modern society as they are in *defending* how gender roles have been defined in the past. It's all too common for Christians to assume that the particular gender roles of their culture are God's ideal. Persons fall into this trap when they impute their cultural expectations to Scripture. A second error is to take *descriptions* of gender roles during biblical times and argue that those descriptions are *normative* for all cultures.

The early men's movement found its authority in structuralism, which is but a pragmatic form of cultural relativism. There is no masculinity or femininity; what we take to be maleness and femaleness are mere reflections of the cultural scripts developed in our society.

The new men's movement seeks a normative basis for ideal manhood in the life experience of men themselves. This they do by clinical analysis of men's dreams and daydreams, and by the collective wisdom of mythology.

As we can see, the traditionalists and the new men's movement are similar in seeking a normative ideal. They both criticize the early men's movement as failing to provide an ideal on which men can begin to build a new manhood. But traditionalists fault the new men's movement for blurring "natural" distinctions between masculinity and femininity. Traditionalists tend to view males' attempt to "get in touch with their feminine side" as regressive rather than progressive. Meanwhile, the new men's movement faults the traditionalists for being satisfied with, and defending, a stunted view of masculinity.

I find merit in each of the models of masculinity I've discussed. I am sympathetic to traditionalists' desire to preserve a distinction between males and females; I also agree that the early men's movement's negation and relativizing of male-female difference was less than helpful.

But I'm also sympathetic to the early men's movement, for I find the "soft male" more appealing than the macho excesses of traditional masculinity. I think Bly and other critics of the early men's movement fail to credit many of its members for their attempts to develop a balanced view of masculinity. The strong and the rational were emphasized along with the soft and the emotional as desirable male characteristics.

I appreciate the desire within the new men's movement to illuminate an image of a fuller masculinity—a masculinity that allows men to be both strong and vulnerable, hard and soft, rational and emotional. But I don't want to give half of what I consider true masculinity away by calling it femininity. I claim vulnerability, softness and emotionality as *masculine* characteristics and not just the feminine side of a male's personhood. While I understand what Bly means when he says that we need more "male mothering," I don't want to label caring and nurture as feminine. What we need is more male fathering—including the *masculine* characteristics of tenderness, nurture and sensitivity.

A Critique of the New Male

The thinkers who have developed the ideal of the new male offer many genuine insights. Some Christians will reject their view of masculinity because mythology rather than Scripture is the source of their wisdom. But this in and of itself is not a good enough reason to reject the new male. God's Word, the Bible, is Christians' basis of authority; but we must recognize that God respects human beings so much that he lets them discover insights and truths apart from his written Word. The discoveries in the scientific laboratory and the clinician's office should not be negated merely because a scriptural proof-text can not be found to corroborate these "secular" insights. We Christians must recognize that all truth is God's truth, and from God's point of view there is no secular-sacred dichotomy.

In offering a critique of the new male, I will attempt to determine whether the movement's teachings are contrary to, corroborated by or consistent with Scripture. Some Christians use the Bible as a sword to categorize ideas as either "contrary to" or "corroborated by" Scripture. But God did not intend Scripture to be an exhaustive statement of all truth and wisdom. Secular wisdom that is neither "contrary to" nor "directly corroborated by" Scripture may be *consistent* with Scripture.

If it can be granted that truth and insight can be found outside of Scripture, then the task for responsible Christians is to examine information and ideas from extrabiblical sources in the light of scriptural truth. Mythology from the variety of cultures around the world includes both wisdom and nonsense. To their credit, the leaders of the new men's movement have attempted to use clinical observations to support insights gained from mythology. But ultimately, these thinkers are handicapped because they have no objective criteria to discern wisdom from nonsense.

When I examine the blueprint for the new male in the light of scriptural wisdom, I find many insights that are corroborated. Christians could do much worse than to base a biblical model of manhood upon the four archetypes of king, warrior, magician and lover.

Jesus is the perfect example of the kingly man. As the true king, Jesus stands in stark contrast to King Herod. The fearful and hate-driven tyrant who ordered the death of thousands of Hebrew babies is a vivid example of a shadow king. The kingly qualities of regenerativity and generosity can be seen in the life of Jesus. He had great power, but he used it for others—he was a man for other people. Jesus manifests the kingly energy of blessing others throughout the accounts of Matthew, Mark, Luke and John.

Although Jesus is known as the man of peace, he also demonstrates mature warrior qualities in his stand against the evils and injustices of his day. Indeed, Scripture as a whole has room for the warrior archetype. Notice the persistent strength of the warrior imagery in Paul's writings: "Therefore take up the whole armor of God, so that you may be able to withstand on that evil day, and having done everything, to stand firm" (Eph 6:13).

The new-male definition of the shadow warrior as one who lacks a commitment to a good greater than himself is also consistent with biblical wisdom. The difference is in the object of that faith commitment. The new-male commitment seems to entail general altruism: life must be lived for an ideal or good beyond oneself. The Christian warrior, however, is committed to God through the person of Jesus Christ.

It's unfortunate that "magician" is used as a masculine archetype in the men's movement. Magicians are mentioned sixteen times in the Bible, and in all instances they are persons who draw upon spiritual powers that are opposed to the one true God. Magicians, along with sorcerers, enchanters and astrologers, were called upon by Pharaoh and King Nebuchadnezzar to counter the power of God channeled through Moses and Daniel, respectively.

Yet Moore and Gillette's magician archetype represents knowledge, wisdom and reflective thought. So within the Christian context the magician might best correspond to the role of the Holy Spirit in the life of a believer. New-male writings describe the magician as the reflective, introverted side of the extroversive warrior. Similarly, as the Christian warrior yields to the control of the Holy Spirit, he will grow in the wisdom and knowledge of God. To be useful in a Christian context, the magician archetype must be reframed to represent the wisdom and power of God that are available to every believer.

There is plenty of room for the lover archetype in a Christian model of manhood. Jesus was a profound lover when he wept for Jerusalem, when he wept at the tomb of Lazarus and when he took the sorrows of the world upon himself. The man under the influence of the lover goes beyond the bounds of conventional law and order for the sake of love. This is exemplified by Jesus' choosing to heal the physically afflicted on the sabbath.

The Bible is full of illustrations and examples that would support the lover as an integral part of Christian manhood. In Christian tradition, however, the pleasures of the senses have often been frowned upon. Sometimes the spirit has been equated with good, and the physical and sensual with evil. Reading the Psalms or the Song of Solomon might help restore our appreciation of the lusty lover of the Bible.

Toward a Christian Model of Manhood

Modern men have been willing to accept as normative a view of masculinity that is based on mythology. The king, warrior, magician and lover archetypes arouse an intuitive response within us—intuitions that had been dampened by our rationalistic, scientific age. Our inner beings hunger for more than objectively calculated rational answers to life's questions. The richness of mythology partially meets that need.

But I also believe that men are open to mythology because modern society has lost the anchorage it once had—which included biblical teaching. Part of the blame for this must fall upon the Christian community. We have devoted more energy to developing a privatized, personal version of Christianity than we have to mining the richness of Scripture to provide answers to the moral and ethical questions of our day. I believe that more than anything else, modern men need a Christian model of manhood.

I've attempted to show that the four masculine archetypes used within the new men's movement do find correspondence in Scripture. Now I intend to go further, trying to fill out a model of masculinity based on Scripture. We'll look at Genesis, and then at the Gospel narratives. Finally, we'll examine the importance of *embodiment* in developing a Christian model of manhood.

Jesus provided us with a perfect model of Christian manhood. Although he was totally God, he was also totally man. And he lived a life of perfection, totally submitted to his Father's will. It could be argued that Jesus' humanity could also be the basis for building an authentic image of womanhood; yet this would not make it wrong to use Jesus as a model for authentic manhood. That will be our goal.

After the Fall

We read in Genesis 1:27 that "God created humankind in his image; in the image of God he created them; male and female he created them." One important implication of this verse is that God created male and female as distinct human beings. There are two ways to be human— as a male or as a female. But we are left to determine exactly what that means and how such differences are to be lived out by a particular male or female.

If we examine the Genesis account of Adam and Eve before the Fall, we find little that would help us define male-female differences. In the past some Christians believed they found support for male dominance and female subordination in Genesis 2:18, which reads, "The LORD God said, 'It is not good that the man should be alone. I will make him a helper as his partner.' " But we need to know that the root word that is here translated as "helper" is found fifteen other times in the Old Testament, *always in reference to God.* Needless to say, it would be a gross misinterpretation of Scripture to think of God as subordinate to humankind because the Bible says that he is our helper.

A stronger case may be made for male-female differences from what Genesis says about the effect of the Fall upon Adam and Eve. For this discussion, I rely heavily on the work of Mary Stewart Van Leeuwen (1990: chapter 2).

Adam and Eve's life in the Garden was good, as they were in need of nothing. All that grew in the Garden was available to them, except the fruit from the tree of the knowledge of good and evil. Adam and Eve were told that if they ate this fruit they would die. Genesis 3:6 tells us, however, that Eve took and ate of the forbidden fruit. Next, she gave some of the fruit to her husband, and he ate it as well.

At one level, Eve and Adam's sins were identical—they both ate the forbidden fruit. Some of the consequences were also identical—their eyes were opened, they realized that they were naked and they felt shame.

At another level, however, each of them sinned in a distinctive way. For her part, Eve went beyond what God had given her and transgressed God's dominion. Her sin was a violation of the *dominion* that was hers. For his part, Adam sinned in response to Eve's request that he participate with her in the eating of the fruit. God's morality called for Adam to remain separate from his wife in this request, to not participate with her in the sin. By uniting with his wife, Adam violated the bounds of healthy *relationship*.

Later in Genesis 3, we read of the consequences of Eve and Adam's sin. They shared three consequences: expulsion from the Garden; struggle and pain in reproducing and feeding their offspring; and death.

For our purposes, though, the most important consequences of the Fall have to do with the curses that Eve and Adam did not share. Here we can see a relationship between the nature of their particular sins and the nature of the punishment specifically given to each. For overstepping God's boundary of dominion, Eve's punishment was that she would be *dominated* by Adam. To Eve God said, "Your desire will be for your husband, and he will rule over you" (3:16). Many have interpreted this sentence to mean that God *intends* (desires) for Adam to lord it over his wife—and that Christian men today should dominate their wives as well. Within the context, however, God's statement is better understood as a consequence that will come from the curse placed upon Adam as well as Eve. For overstepping God's boundary of proper relationship, Adam's punishment was that he would seek to dominate Eve, against God's intention for marriage.

The consequence of the curse for Adam was that in seeking to dominate, he would thwart closeness and intimacy. One consequence of the Fall for all males, then, is difficulty in achieving intimacy in relationships.

It's worth noting that this difference in consequences for Adam and Eve corresponds to psychological research: females have been found to be more relational and open to social connectedness, while males are more oriented to differentiation and separateness (Gilligan 1982).

As a result of the Fall, men have a built-in (congenital) tendency to attempt to dominate in personal relationships. Although we must begin with this understanding of the basic nature of masculinity, we should consider well before claiming dominance as a healthy tendency that God desires. To better grasp God's ideal for manhood, we need to examine the life of the man Jesus Christ.

Jesus as a Model for Manhood

Two surprisingly contrasting images of Jesus the man have been perpetuated through the history of the Christian church. At times Jesus has so been feminized (based on cultural definitions of femininity) that he bears little resemblance to a real man. This is the "meek and mild" Jesus, ever ready to turn the other cheek when challenged. Such a passive image of Jesus can especially be seen in pre-Renaissance Christian art.

At other times Jesus has been masculinized to fit a cultural ideal of a savior who, like a Western sheriff, was physically strong and stood up for what was right. This version presents us with a flaming revolutionary who is defiantly standing against the existing order. Similarly, in their eagerness to make Christianity appeal to men, some contemporary evangelists portray Jesus as a tough, rugged "man's man."

Instead of simply accepting one of these images, let's turn to Scripture. Surveying the life of Jesus, we find a man who experienced a wide range of emotions. The most dominant emotional characteristic we see in Jesus is his compassion or love. The Gospels report numerous occasions when Jesus showed both internal feelings (he loved and pitied) and external action (he helped the needy). He was compassionate toward the blind man, lepers, the bereaved widow, the woman at the well and Lazarus' sisters. His love for the multitudes is also seen in his acts of feeding the hungry and healing the sick, and in his concern for the lost, whom he described as "sheep without a shepherd."

Jesus' compassion was sometimes expressed in sorrow. He wept over Jerusalem because of the unbelief of its people. When he saw Mary, Martha and their friends weeping at Lazarus's death, he, too, wept. Preparing to heal the deaf and dumb man, Jesus looked up to heaven with a deep sigh. When the Pharisees sought to test him by asking for a sign from heaven, he sighed deeply.

At other times Jesus' love moved him to express great joy. When the seventy whom he had sent out to witness returned rejoicing, we are told that Jesus "rejoiced in the Holy Spirit" (Lk 10:21). He also speaks of joy in heaven when just one sinner repents. Jesus tells his disciples that if they abide in his love, his joy will also be in them (Jn 15:10-11). The love of Jesus for his disciples can also be seen in his statements to them just prior to his death: "So you have pain now; but I will see you again, and your hearts will rejoice, and no one will take your joy from you" (Jn 16:22). Praying to his heavenly Father, Jesus says that he has spoken his truth so that his followers might be filled with joy (Jn 17:13).

Although Jesus was meek, mild and tender, he was also capable of anger and indignation. In a world under the curse of sin, Jesus responded angrily to human beings' cruelty, hardness of heart, unbelief and to hypocrisy. The same Jesus who said, "Let the little children come to me" (Lk 18:16), drove out those who bought and sold animals in the temple and upset the tables of the money changers. Jesus' anger at the hypocrisy of the Pharisees can be seen when he called them "white-washed tombs . . . full of the bones of the dead and of all kinds of filth" and "you snakes, you brood of vipers" (Mt 23:27, 33). His language was equally severe when he called Herod a "fox" (Lk 13:32), hearers of his message "swine" (Mt 7:6) and false prophets "ravenous wolves" (Mt 7:15).

Jesus possessed a wide range of emotions and was harmoniously complete in his human individuality. He also had the full range of human needs and appetites—he hungered, thirsted, was weary, knew physical pain and pleasure, slept, grew in knowledge, wept, suffered and died. All that is human manifested itself in perfect proportion and balance in Jesus Christ. He was emotionally mature and able to freely express his emotions to himself and to others.

If Jesus lived on earth in modern times, how might we classify him according to traditional masculine and feminine ideals? I would encourage you to take this question seriously and try to answer it by doing the following assessment. First, find a pencil and sheet of paper. Then, based on your knowledge of Jesus' life, list one-word descriptions of his personal characteristics. Give yourself about five minutes to compile your list *before* you read the next paragraph.

When you have completed your list of adjectives for Jesus, reflect on how masculinity and femininity are traditionally defined. Go back over the words on your list, one by one, assessing whether each fits the traditional masculine ideal or the traditional feminine ideal. If you think the adjective is "masculine," simply write an *M* in front of the word. If you think the adjective best fits the traditional feminine ideal, write an *F* in front of it. If the word does not describe either gender more than the other, skip to the next word.

Finally, total up the number of "M" words and compare that sum to the number of "F" words. This will give you an idea of how masculine or feminine you think Jesus was during his time here on earth.

In giving this assignment in a number of classes and men's retreats, I have found the numbers of masculine and feminine adjectives used to describe Jesus to be surprisingly equivalent. When Christians examine the biblical record, the picture of Jesus that emerges is not one of a man who was masculine or feminine according to our cultural standards. Rather, Jesus seems to have embodied the best of the characteristics that we divide and assign to males on the one hand and females on the other.

A masculinized or feminized image of Jesus is not supported by the scriptural narratives. Taken alone, each view is incomplete. But taken together, they suggest the rich depth that characterized Jesus' human life. So we men need to turn to Jesus to find liberation from the sterile, restricted definitions of manhood that are prevalent in modern culture.

Turning now to what I call "male embodiment," I hope to show that characteristics such as kindness, gentleness and tenderness are not merely part of our "feminine side," as the new men's movement would have us believe, but are an inherent part of masculinity.

Male Embodiment

Our bodies can also contribute to our model of masculinity. God created men in a physical body with bodily parts that are uniquely male. James Nelson (1988) suggests that if we are in tune with our embodiment we will find that God has given us clues to appropriate masculine behavior. In creating the male body distinct from the female body, God designed men to experience life in a masculine way. Every male must live out his manhood within his body.[1]

Pinocchio experienced life through one organ, his nose, which grew longer whenever he told a lie. And men often accept the lie that the most valuable aspects of masculinity are represented by the size of one organ—their erect penis. Nelson believes that while men value *phallus*, the genital erect, they devalue *penis*, the genital at rest. Realizing this helps us see how our society glorifies certain aspects of masculinity while devaluing others.

The phallus has come to symbolize masculinity. To be erect is to have strength and determination, while to be limp is to be weak and wishy-washy. It is better for a man to be big than small, to ride tall in the saddle rather than slumped over, to be hard rather than soft. Just look at the tall, straight monuments men build for themselves—unambiguous phallus symbols. A real man drives himself toward a goal, never faltering, because he is confident that he can penetrate any obstacle.

The male emphasis upon phallus goes along with the near-exclusion of penis. The result is that men have limited themselves to one mode of expressing themselves. It is as if men had the capacity to walk on both legs, but choose instead to get around on just one. It is like a two-piston engine running on just one. It's as if men were by nature bilingual, but

---

[1]Many of the insights in this section are based on James Nelson's excellent book *The Intimate Connection: Male Sexuality, Masculine Spirituality* (1988).

chose to speak only one language. We have chosen to handicap ourselves.

Men need to get in touch with the other half of their masculinity, which is a part of their male embodiment. The two-legged, two-piston or bilingual male can embrace strength and tenderness, hardness and softness, bigness and smallness, tenseness and relaxation, without identifying any of these characteristics as feminine. They are all natural masculine modes to be experienced as complementary to each other. In fact, strength, hardness, bigness and tenseness are meaningless except as contrasted to tenderness, softness, smallness and relaxation. To identify the latter qualities as feminine is not only to give away natural masculine parts of us, but also to connote that men have to learn a foreign language. This is not the case at all. Learning to be tender, soft and relaxed is not learning to be feminine; it's reclaiming the masculinity that we've been taught to suppress.

Nelson points out a significant irony in the way men refer to certain male parts—their testicles. The very part of the male body that is used as a metaphor for toughness and strength is also the part that's considered most vulnerable. When we wish to identify a man as strong and tough, we say, "He's got balls." But also when we are egging someone on to attack a man in a vulnerable place, we cry, "Kick him in the balls!" The testicles—uniquely male parts—are equally identified as the place of strength and the place of vulnerability.

Does it seem a contradiction? It's not. The contradiction is only in the mind of the one who wants to define masculinity as strength without vulnerability, toughness without tenderness. Unless a man has "balls" he is neither strong nor vulnerable. The embodiment of masculinity is to have balls—to have strength and tenderness as complementary *masculine* characteristics.

Claiming Our Full Masculinity

It's important that we reclaim our full masculinity. Jesus was a model of that full manhood. Jesus was just as much a man when he wept and showed tenderness as when he was driving the money changers out of the temple. A Christian model of masculinity includes hardness, strength, determination, rationality and all the characteristics identified with traditional masculinity, and tenderness, nurture, caring, emotionality and other characteristics traditionally identified as feminine. One set of characteristics is not our masculine side and the other our feminine. Both are a part of our true, complete manhood.

When the Bible speaks of Christian temperament, it fails to make a distinction between males and females. Paul writes in Galatians 5:22, "The fruit of the Spirit is love, joy, peace, patience, kindness, generosity, faithfulness, gentleness, and self-control." In our culture, all these attributes are typically considered to be feminine. On the basis of these verses, I would argue that not only should males and females be more alike, but that males need to cultivate the Christian qualities that have traditionally been defined as feminine.

Although God has created us for relationship, our first impulse may be to seek distance and separateness. We need a vision of a redeemed manhood that chooses human connectedness as a complement to our need for separateness. Many of the issues dealt with in the following chapters have to do with this important need for males to be connected—to our wives, our children, our fathers and mothers, our sisters and brothers, our male friends, our female friends and even our enemies.

PART III

MALE ISSUES

5

MALE INEXPRESSIVENESS

Barrier to Intimacy

Another thing I learned—if *you* cry, the audience won't. A man can cry for his horse, for his dog, for another man, but he cannot cry for a woman. A strange thing. He can cry at the death of a friend or a pet. But where he's supposed to be boss, with his children or wife, something like that, he better hold 'em back and let *them* cry.

JOHN WAYNE

I grew up in a small rural community in the heart of California's fertile San Joaquin Valley; my roots stretch back to the Swedish immigrants who settled in this community. I can recall as a boy overhearing two Swedish farmers as they talked about their wives. What sticks in my mind most is one Swedish-accented comment: "You know, I love my wife so much that sometimes I can hardly keep from telling her."

I also remember my first day at kindergarten. During recess I was demonstrating to my new classmates my skill in pumping myself to great heights on the playground swing. I remember the pride I felt—until my left hand slipped and I suffered a humiliating free fall, crashing to the ground with a painful thud.

I don't know which hurt the most, the physical impact when I hit the ground, or the blow to my pride because of this embarrassing mishap. I do remember that *I didn't cry!* And this feat of emotional self-control rescued me from further humiliation in front of my peers. Picking myself up, I declared, "That didn't hurt!" and proceeded to strut away as I fought back the tears. I had already learned one rule about being a man: *Feelings of love, tenderness, affection, sorrow, grief or hurt are not to be expressed.*

The traditional definition of manhood encompasses not only what "real" men should do but also what a real man should *not* do. Inexpressiveness is a stereotypical male characteristic that traditionally has been defined in negative terms. Simply put, an expressive male is one who has feelings and verbally expresses them, while an inexpressive male does not verbally express his feelings.

While some inexpressive males believe that they have no feelings to express, most men are verbally inexpressive because they believe it is the way men should be. Given the current redefinition of gender roles, an increasing number of men may want to express their feelings, but because of past as well as current restrictive socialization, they're still uncomfortable doing it.

It's especially ironic that the very feelings that ought to be most effortless and pleasurable to express, such as "I love you," wind up being the most difficult. It makes sense that we'd want to avoid saying "I hate you" to someone. But "I love you" should flow with a natural ease from our inner reservoir of feelings.

We know that nothing would make those we love happier than to hear an expression of our love. And yet we feel strangely uncomfortable just thinking about communicating love. It's so easy to express passionate thoughts and feelings about politics, or sports, or even religion. But to express our love freely to another person—well, that's something else! Why do we need to talk about that? Shouldn't some things just be taken for granted?

It isn't that men don't have feelings of love. We do feel love toward our wives, our children, our parents, our close friends. We do not doubt that the feelings are there; in fact, these are often the most certain feelings we have. But to communicate those feelings verbally is especially difficult.

At a deeper level, men's discomfort with communicating love may reflect the risk of being close to another. Perhaps as a young boy the man had sought closeness with his father, but experienced abandonment when his father was unable to respond with tenderness.

The Man of Action

Men and women specialize in different modes of communication. The basis of this difference seems to be present in infancy. While female babies are more attracted to human faces and respond more to nuances of facial expression, males are more attracted to the movement of objects and are better at manipulating them. In early childhood girls develop a ready connection between feelings and their expression in words, while boys are more likely to express their feelings through their actions. So it seems that from day one males have a genetic predisposition to act out rather than verbalize their feelings.

Feelings between people can be communicated in a number of ways—through body language, overt physical behavior, symbolic gestures and written language. There may even be some truth to the axiom that "actions speak louder than words." Our eyes, lips, face, posture and general body movement all do a great deal to express what we are feeling. The wife and children of a verbally inexpressive male may become skilled readers of body language, interpreting how he is feeling without a word being spoken. One eight-year-old girl was asked how she knew her daddy was mad; she replied, "When he gets a frown on his face and starts stamping around the house like he's pounding nails into the floor with his feet!"

But there's a problem: although body language can express feelings, a man who uses it as his primary avenue of expression will often give off ambiguous messages. This, of course, increases the chances for misinterpretation and misunderstanding.

Men also attempt to communicate through more overt physical means—positively through a hug, a kiss or a pat on the back, or negatively through hitting, pushing or shoving. A number of years ago I was studying marriage relationships among Greeks in Cyprus. One of the questions I asked the wives was how often their husbands said "I love you." Every wife reported that her husband never said it, and one wife in her thirties explained, "Greek men are men of action, not men of words!" Most of the wives I interviewed said that their husbands did express love physically, but they wished their husbands would also *tell* them of their love.

Men may also attempt to communicate their feelings through symbolic gestures: giving a dozen roses, a card, two tickets to Hawaii—or, negatively, "forgetting" an important event, or refusing to listen or to participate in an activity. The gift (or lack of a gift) and the participation (or refusal) represent feelings that are not spoken. Symbolic gestures are a normal and expected part of most close relationships.

Some men who have difficulty expressing themselves out loud become adept at expressing feelings through writing. Love and appreciation can be expressed through a letter, a poem or a song. Although they are disastrous as art, my wife cherishes the love poems I have written to her.

It's often easier for men to express love in writing than in verbal interaction. Most intimate relationships would probably profit from attempts to express love in writing. Many women will still want and need the intimacy of speech, but writing one's tender feelings may be a step toward expressing them orally.

Is the male model of communication sufficient? Many men hope that their actions will be enough to convey their deep feelings. But I believe that oral communication has two advantages that are not combined in any of the nonverbal modes of communication: it is *precise* and *personal.*

Body language, overt physical behavior and symbolic gestures may be personal, but they lack precision. Body language can be misread— "What does that gleam in his eye really mean?" Physical expressions can be misinterpreted—"Is he interested in me as a person, or just in my body?" Symbolic acts may be questioned—"Why did he send me these flowers? What has he done now?"

Although written communication is highly precise, it's not as direct and personal as speech. Expressing feelings through writing makes a simultaneous exchange of communication difficult. Letters and poems are usually intended for reading while the writer is not present.

I'm certainly not saying that oral communication is immune to misinterpretation, or that speech is always sincere. I'm only suggesting that feelings of love, tenderness, anger, frustration, disappointment, sadness and grief can be communicated most completely, personally and precisely through speech. Expressing these feelings out loud brings us closer to the experience of true intimacy.

Personal feelings are so complex and multidimensional that they may be compared to the many facets of a finely cut diamond. The diamond can be appreciated in its entirety only from many angles. Each angle will show a different facet of the diamond's loveliness, and yet the diamond is a whole. The depth and dimensions of personal feelings are best communicated by body language, physical expressions, symbolic gestures, writing *and* speech—all of them. Men who do not express their feelings out loud are like multilingual persons who do not communicate in their primary language.

The Cost of Inexpressiveness

Male inexpressiveness is no trivial problem; it's a real tragedy for wives, for children and most especially for men themselves. Think of the wife who, year after year, never hears the words "I love you." Consider the discouragement in the child who is never told, "Fine work, I'm proud of you." And think of the tragedy of the man himself, crippled by an inability to express an important part of himself—his warm and tender feelings for other people.

It is both physically and psychologically unhealthy for a man not to release and express emotions. The inability to cry and express emotions is related to poorer overall physical health (Downey 1984). We now know that keeping emotions bottled up is related to the fact that men more than women have ulcers, high blood pressure, stomach disorders, a shorter life span and a number of other physical and psychosomatic problems. James Harrison (1978:81) concluded that "a critical reading of presently available evidence confirms that male role socialization contributes to the higher mortality of men."

Psychologically, holding in emotions can result in a man's being out of touch with himself. Bottled-up feelings are unhealthy physically and psychologically, but they also work themselves out *behaviorally*. People who deny or push down their emotions often behave in ineffective, unhealthy and hurtful ways. Suppressed anger at a spouse, for example, may be vented unreasonably toward another person.

Articulating feelings helps us become aware of our emotions so that we can learn how to deal with them. When we don't articulate what we feel, it's hard to know what the feelings are. Just as talking over a problem helps us understand it, so articulating emotions forces us to conceptualize them.

Inexpressiveness keeps many men from developing intimate, meaningful relationships. As Samuel Osherson (1986:2) summarizes his findings from interviews with 370 men, "Many men showed confusion about the intimacy issues in their lives, particularly with wives, children, and their own parents." Research has also found a correlation between poorly adjusted marriages and husbands who have difficulty expressing their feelings (Balswick 1988).

Even more serious, however, is the evidence that inexpressive males are more likely to resort to violence and physical abuse with their children and wives. The man who lacks assertiveness and allows his feelings to be bottled up may well resort to acts of aggression. Men who effectively give release to their emotions don't need to act in violence.

Fatherhood brings with it a whole complex of demands for inexpressive men. To begin with, his wife, who is now a mother, needs even more emotional support and expressiveness from him than she did before. The mother may be spending long hours meeting the new baby's rather taxing physical and emotional needs, but the infant can't express positive emotions toward her in return. It can be expected that she'll turn to her husband for encouragement to help her meet the infant's emotional demands until she can replenish her own spent emotional resources. She may also feel insecure about handling her new tasks of infant care, and needs reassurance from her husband. Also, she has just gone through pregnancy, and now infant care leaves her little time and energy for personal beautification; she may long for reassurances that she is still attractive and loved.

Clearly, the greatest demands for the new father may have to do more with his wife's needs than with the child. The emotionally inexpressive male may be unable to respond to his wife's emotional needs.

Given the current redefinition of gender roles, fathers are being asked to do more to nurture their children. They are expected to express emotions of tenderness, gentleness and affection to their little ones. If inexpressive men have male children, these demands may be especially acute in the early years. Young boys may need and want spoken affection just as much as daughters do. Inexpressive fathers may be afraid their sons won't grow into "men" if they treat them tenderly and gently. The irony is that boys who are most secure in their masculinity are ones who have experienced warm and intimate relationships with their fathers. Fathers who avoid intimacy with their sons are reproducing inexpressiveness and insecurity in their sons.

Although the new father's emotional capacities may have grown through his practice in expressing tender feelings toward his wife, those capacities may still be too limited. The first years of marriage sometimes serve as a lull between the turmoil of the single inexpressive male and the demands of fatherhood. If inexpressive males do not make major strides in opening up their feelings, their fathering will suffer greatly.

Why Can't Men Express Their Feelings?

It is not that men can't express their feelings, but that they have a hard time expressing *certain kinds* of feelings. Boys growing up in America learn very early that a "real man" doesn't vent his tender feelings. In learning to be a man, the boy comes to value expressions of "masculinity" and devalue expressions of "femininity." Masculinity is expressed largely through physical courage, toughness, competitiveness and aggressiveness, whereas femininity is expressed in gentleness, expressiveness and responsiveness.

When a young boy begins to express his emotions through crying, his parents are quick to reproach him: "You're a big boy, and big boys don't cry," or "Don't be such a sissy," or "Try to be a man about it." When his sister hugs her mother, she hugs back; when he hugs his father, his father stiffens and pulls away.

Parents often use the expression "He's all boy" in reference to their son, and they are talking about behavior that expresses aggressiveness—

getting into mischief, getting dirty. He tracks mud across the rug, breaks a lamp, gets into a fight with a neighboring child; we sigh, but say with some pride, "He's all boy." Parents don't apply this description to behavior that expresses affection, tenderness or love (like writing a poem or picking wildflowers for his mother). Anger, boisterous humor, competitive or athletic enthusiasm and similar emotions are deemed to be "manly" and acceptable; but "feminine" emotions (tenderness, compassion, sentimentality, gentleness, verbal affection, soft-heartedness and the like) are clearly to be avoided. What parents are really telling their son is that a real man does not express his feelings.

I have spent much of the last twenty years conducting research in an attempt to understand why men have difficulty expressing their tender feelings. Let me summarize here what I have written in my book *The Inexpressive Male* (Balswick 1988). There is some biological evidence that males have a harder time than females in making a connection between feelings and the expression of those feelings in words. But this evidence explains only the origin of the expressive difference between males and females, not why the differences are often so great. I suggest that parents inadvertently accentuate tendencies that already exist in their very young children. Such tendencies are *labeled* by parents, and labeling a child prompts him or her to act in accordance with the label. Any inborn tendency a boy may have toward inexpressiveness becomes part of a self-fulfilling prophecy: his parents' expectation that he won't express his feelings actually helps to bring about inexpressiveness. As the expectation that males can't express their feelings becomes a societal norm, people come to consider it only "normal" that men can't express their feelings.

Boys who are parented by mothers more than by fathers, and especially those who have cold and distant relationships with their fathers, can be expected to be most inexpressive. At the simplest level, boys who see that their fathers are emotionally distant and inexpressive will copy this behavior. At a more complex level, boys with cold, distant fathers will be less sure of their masculinity, and as a result they will conform to an extreme form of male inexpressiveness. Masculine insecurity causes them to "prove" they are real men by not showing their feelings. On the other hand, where there are intimate and expressive relationships between fathers and sons, the sons will accept expressiveness as part of healthy masculinity.

Once developed as a normative part of the male gender role, inexpressiveness is difficult to undo. Not only does inexpressiveness become a part of males' self-concept, but it also becomes a social expectation, reinforced by the patterns and institutions of our culture. For this reason, later in this chapter I will suggest that it's not only individual males who need to change; we need to bring change into the larger systems and structures of modern society.

Men's Need for Intimacy

Men need to be liberated from the emotional hang-ups that prevent them from developing intimate relationships. The stigma of appearing too emotional, too expressive and too open and vulnerable about personal things has kept many men tied to traditional masculinity. Although increased emotional expressiveness is not a panacea for the difficulty men now experience in trying to redefine masculinity and gender roles, expressive change can have vast benefits and rewards for them, their families and friends, and society in general.

The benefits of increased expressiveness for men themselves are both physical and psychological. Physically, releasing tears and learning to express emotions can relieve stress and improve one's health. Psychologically, the ability to recognize feelings will enhance self-awareness and provide a release from denial and repression. Articulating feelings is one way to get a better understanding of problems; with this understanding, one can choose constructive action to solve problems, rather than struggling under the weight of vague depression and anxiety.

A second benefit of increased male expressiveness has to do with the quality of love relationships. Newborns' strong need for nurture and overt expressions of love is never outgrown. In fact, as children mature from infancy to adulthood, they may even develop an increased need for physical expressions of love. A father's expressions of love to his child leaves the child with a heartfelt conviction that he or she is precious and valuable. His expressions of love also prepare the child to receive love and to give love to others—to build healthy, ongoing relationships. Increased male expressiveness will contribute to children's emotional health—and fathers will have the reward of stronger relationships with their children.

Men who learn to express their feelings to the ones they love will experience vastly deeper and richer relationships. Intimate relationships are based on *commitment* and maintained by *communication*. Although emotions are involved in love, more than anything else, love is a commitment that involves rights and responsibilities. From the recipient's point of view, rights are involved; from the giver's point of view, responsibility is involved. True love relationships are always reciprocal and mutual—they are two-way, not one-way. Each person gives and takes.

In the same way that mutual commitment is the *basis* of a love relationship, mutual communication is the *process* by which a love relationship is maintained and enhanced. A love relationship does not grow when communication goes only one direction—for example, when only the wife attempts to express personal feelings. At best, one-way communication may simply keep the relationship alive. And most of us expect more than that from marriage. Companionship is at the heart of our modern understanding of marriage; we expect intimacy, and one-way communication can't sustain intimacy. Wives who desire greater intimacy may make valiant efforts to get their husbands to express their feelings. When husbands do not change, and thus the wives' intimacy needs are not being satisfied, the end result may be divorce.

When an inexpressive husband becomes more expressive, it can have dramatic effects in many areas of his life. His relationships grow and deepen. The insecurity that comes from not knowing where one stands in a relationship is transformed into deep feelings of security. He no longer needs to resort to devious, manipulative behavior to try to evoke some kind of positive response in others. He finds that expression of love is the cement that maintains intimacy.

Can Women Help?

A woman can begin to help a man become more expressive by being expressive herself. There are women who have difficulty expressing their feelings—although not nearly as many as men. By giving something of her own spirit, by revealing her own feelings, a woman can go a long way toward encouraging a man to open up too.

Being open herself helps in one surprising way. Curiously, a man who doesn't express himself easily sometimes fails simply because he doesn't quite know how. He literally doesn't know what words to use. Those who are used to being expressive find that the words roll out easily; those who aren't, however, may not be able to find the words at all. There are many ways to say what we feel; when a wife says, "Thanks for cheering me on last night when I needed it," or "I really feel close to you sometimes, like today," or just "I love you," she is, in fact, giving her husband a vocabulary lesson.

It will also help for a woman to assure her husband that she has no doubts about his "maleness." She can do this quite simply by telling him occasionally what a good man he is. She may also encourage him by saying something like "It takes a strong man to show tenderness and be gentle. It makes me feel secure with you." The more he feels that she is seeing him as "solidly male," the more he can allow himself the "weakness" of opening up his feelings to her.

Another key is for a woman to base her security on God instead of her husband or boyfriend. Firmly rooted in God's love, she can be secure enough to contain her man's feelings of insecurity. With God as her main source of strength, she will not need to pressure her lover to keep up a façade of strength.

Once a man begins to open up a little, a woman must be encouraging and supportive. This isn't always easy. Suppose she asks him about his job, and suddenly, for the first time, he blurts out that he hates it and wants to quit. Understandably, she may panic and say, "Oh, you can't do that! Think of the children." But it would be far better to say something like, "From what you tell me about it, I don't blame you; I'd hate it too." Few men will simply quit their jobs and leave their families in the lurch. If the wife is calmly supportive and willing to listen, she can work with her husband to help him find a happier career.

Change won't happen unless it comes from within a man. A caring woman can help facilitate change, but a man must want to become expressive of his feelings before it will happen. The male who is resistant to change may be in a codependent relationship: his wife may be an unknowing co-conspirator who does his "emotional work" for him. A caring wife must be sensitive to the possibility that her husband has become dependent upon her to identify what he is feeling. She may have a need to be needed and may unconsciously not want him to grow emotionally. The wife who truly helps her husband will empower him toward greater responsibility for identifying and expressing his own feelings, rather than letting him continue to be dependent upon her.

Peter, Do You Love Me?

In the last chapter of his Gospel, John gives an account of one of the last exchanges between Jesus and his disciples. Peter and some of the others have been fishing during the night on the Sea of Galilee. They come to shore just as day is breaking, and find Jesus tending a charcoal fire and inviting them to join him for breakfast. After the meal, Jesus turns to Peter and asks him three times, "Do you love me?" Each time Peter replies, "Yes, you know that I love you." We are told that Peter was grieved after Jesus asked him this question for the third time.

Although there is no way to know the mind of Jesus during this encounter, we know that he had a definite reason for posing the same question to Peter three times. It may be more than coincidental that Peter had earlier denied Jesus three times. We have no way of knowing whether Peter had already asked Jesus' forgiveness for his denial. If he had not, perhaps Jesus knew that Peter had a definite need to express these feelings, to reaffirm his love after he had denied it through his words and actions. Soon he would be one of a small group left on this earth to carry on the work Jesus had started. Peter needed a chance to recommit himself to Jesus and affirm his love.

After this conversation, Peter was a changed man. The person who traveled throughout the first-century world telling the good news of Jesus' victory over death bore little resemblance to the person who just a short time earlier had denied his Lord three times.

With the removal of his barrier to intimacy, Peter changed from an intimidated coward to a fearless witness. Many of us men are experiencing barriers to intimacy as well. Many of us have a fear of intimacy, of expressing our love in intimate relationships. Scripture tells us:

There is no fear in love, but perfect love casts out fear; for fear has to do with punishment, and whoever fears has not reached perfection in love. We love because he first loved us. (1 Jn 4:18-19)

6

COMPETITION, AGGRESSION AND WAR

Restraining the Warrior

When women have a voice in national and international affairs, war will cease forever.

AUGUSTA STOWE-GULLEN

H e's a winner!" "He's a real loser!" No two pronouncements can so effectively elicit feelings of self-worth or worthlessness in a man. To be a winner is to be number one, first, on top, the best! Not to win is mediocrity or failure. A major component in the male role is the show of strength, which can take the form of competition, daring adventurousness, aggression, violence or war. Although there are notable exceptions, this pattern of competition, aggression and violence can be found among males in most societies around the world.

Let's examine the place of competition in the male role. Then I will discuss men's tendency to become involved in violence and war.

Competition

From early childhood, boys are indirectly taught to compete against other boys. If girls learn to compete for boys, boys learn to compete not only for girls but also for status and respect. Although the traditional American status symbols include achievement in sports, occupation, education and salary, men can compete at almost anything, and will do so in order to gain status.

Several years ago, I participated in a sensitivity group. We were all encouraged to share our thoughts and feelings openly with the group. I can remember getting caught up in a competitive spirit as other group members shared. When my turn came, I was determined to "outshare" everyone else.

My greatest competitor in this group turned out to be Doug, an athletic coach who, like me, normally had trouble expressing his feelings. But when the name of the game was to share, our inhibitions suddenly evaporated in the promised glory of outsharing everyone else.

After the session ended, Doug and I had a long talk about our involvement in the group and how much competition had been our motivator. This helped us gain a better understanding of ourselves as competitors and the effects it had on our lives, both positive and negative.

The same group brought me a great revelation regarding the negative effect of competition upon nonathletic males. We were sharing how we felt in grade school when it was time to choose up sides to play baseball, basketball, football or some other team sport. Since I excelled in most sports, I had often been nominated to be a team captain responsible for choosing players. My experience seemed positive to me, and I was expecting the other men in the group to tell how these sports had built friendship between themselves and other boys. As we went around the circle, however, I was shocked at what nearly half of the men shared. Their memories were less than positive: they had experienced the choosing of players as the establishment of a pecking order.

Several men said that the process of choosing up sides was their *very worst* memory about grade school. Each of these men told of the fear he had felt that he might be the *last* one chosen. I saw tears well up in the eyes of one man as he explained how humiliated he had felt when he indeed was the last chosen. He could still hear the other boys taunting, "Oh no, we don't have a chance with Harry on our side," and "You take Harry—we don't want him."

Another man spoke of how embarrassing it had been to be chosen *after* the one girl who regularly sought to play with the guys. The humiliation had been so great that he had worked out an ingenious solution. He struck up a bargain with his more athletic buddy, who was usually one of the boys doing the choosing. In exchange for the promise of being chosen at a respectable time, he agreed to help his buddy with his homework.

The pressure upon men to compete successfully is surely one reason that many men identify so strongly with college and professional athletic teams. We may define ourselves as failures in our own competitive endeavors, but we can be winners vicariously through our favorite sports team.

After an athletic contest has been decided, the most predictable chant from supporters of the winning team will be, "We're number one! We're number one!" I suggest that these chants reveal much about men's inner needs to be number one. How else can we understand how close some men come to major depression when "their" team loses? Or the increasingly violent behavior of crowds at sporting events?

Because of fans' violence at a soccer match for the European Cup, which resulted in a number of serious injuries and deaths, teams from England were barred from further competition. To protect opposing fans from one another, iron fences have been built in soccer stadiums in many parts of the world.

Deep in the psyche of many men is an intense need to be a winner. When winning is denied, either directly or vicariously, some men will resort to violence. The ultimate form of violence is war. So let's consider the relationship between masculinity and war.

Fighting like a Man

History shows us quite clearly that "human aggression" is largely *male aggression*. Most of the fighting, terrorism and violence in the world can be understood as desperate attempts by men to confirm their own masculinity. The predictable male response to a threat is a show of toughness, strength, invulnerability and invincibility.

Men's tendency to resort to physical power and aggression may be the major universal barrier to peacemaking in the world today. Can anything be done about this? I believe the answer is a resounding *Yes, men can change!* But before developing this answer, we need to consider a sociobiological explanation that implies that it will be difficult to reduce male aggression.

Male aggression according to sociobiology. Although chapter two presented some basic principles of sociobiology, the explanation of male aggression is usually centered on social evolutionary arguments. It is argued that the goal of human behavior is to increase the chances that genetic lines will survive. Given the differential contribution of males and females to the reproductive process, members of each gender tried to protect their "genetic packages" in different ways. Since females have only a few eggs to be fertilized, investment in any conception is great; they thus sought to "save themselves" for a male who was strong, dependable and likely to help care for their child.

Males, on the other hand, had an unlimited number of sperm, so they could "diversify their investments." In a situation where females controlled sex and reproduction, males would fight one another over access to females. The successful fighters gained access to the females and thus were successful in passing on their genes. The weak (losers) did not get the chance to pass on their genes. So aggressive males spread their genes more effectively than nonaggressive males.

People today, according to this theory, are descendants of strong fighting males and choosy females. Parenthetically, this is also how sociobiologists explain the emergence of the double sexual standard, love and "pair-bonding." For males the cost of sex is negligible, while the potential benefit is great. For females the cost is great, but the potential benefit is small (it takes a great investment of women's time and energy to rear a child into adulthood). Pair-bonding, or marriage, emerged because more offspring survived when *both* parents cared for the child.

Sociobiologists believe that males are genetically "programmed" to be aggressive and to defend their own territory. Many conservative Christians agree that males are programmed to be more aggressive than females, but they reject a social evolutionary explanation of this. They believe that God created males and females different in temperament to correspond to his design for a hierarchically based social order. Within this order, men are designed to provide for the economic needs of family and society and to protect against attacks from outside, while women are designed to provide nurture and care for the socio-emotional needs within the family.

Male aggression according to sociological theory. Since a whole section of chapter two is devoted to sociological explanations of gender differences, I will give only a brief summary here. In general, sociologists cite differences in culturally defined appropriateness in gender roles. These gender roles can be thought of as "sexual scripts": girls and boys are carefully taught their respective gender lines until a firm feminine or masculine identity is established. As traditionally given, the female script calls for an interpersonal orientation—giving nurture, emotional expressiveness, tenderness and care. The male script calls for an instrumental orientation—rational thought, aggressiveness and dominance.

As I stated in chapter two, I believe that *part* of the origin of gender differences in aggression is biological, but *most* of the difference results from socialization. Since much male aggressiveness is learned, I believe that much of it can also be unlearned. But, unlike the social structuralists described in chapter two, I do not believe that it can be completely "socialized out" of men.

A simplistic explanation simply won't work. Conservatives are right in criticizing the naiveté of the "liberal" (social structuralist) view, but I think conservatives, too, are wrong in their fatalistic opinion that men can't change. I believe that aggressiveness toward others is sinful, and that God calls us to build bridges between people and societies who appear to be our enemies. Reconciliation means being "Christ to the world," and it will do far more in the long run to discourage human aggressiveness than pessimistic proclamations that "there will always be wars and rumors of war" as we continue to build bigger and better killing machines.

War, Pride and Shame
From sports to war, men are obsessed with winning, and claiming the honor that goes along with winning. This is vividly illustrated by the glorious homecoming celebrations given to military personnel returning from the Gulf War of early 1990 (Operation Desert Storm). This

response stood in stark contrast to the shame that had been showered on servicemen returning from the Vietnam War. For more than fifteen years, the United States endured the shame of failing to win its war against a much less powerful opponent, North Vietnam. We were Goliath, defeated by little David.

Before the Gulf War, the U.S. government made several impotent attempts in the 1980s to restore its "manhood." First, the United States unleased its military might against the island nation of Grenada. Exactly why Grenada was such a threat to world freedom and democracy is as much a mystery today as it was then. Nevertheless, our political leaders placed great importance upon our victory over Grenada. They tried to convince us that the crucial thing was not whom we defeated, but the fact that *we won.* The Grenada victory proved insufficient, however, to remove the sense of shame that lingered in the soul of masculine America.

The military invasion of Panama in late 1989 was a second attempt to vindicate our manhood. This followed an attempt to paint the drug-dealing dictator Manuel Noriega as a worthy enemy for our military strength. What he lacked in military might was compensated for by the fact that he dared to laugh at U.S. threats and figuratively spat in America's face. While our masculine soul felt good about bringing down such a renegade opponent, the easy victory did little to eradicate our sense of shame.

The perfect opponent. Finally, Saddam Hussein's ruthless invasion of Kuwait offered the perfect opportunity for the United States to vindicate its shame. Never mind that we had been among the Iraqi leader's most loyal supporters during his long war with Iran, nor that the worldwide economic embargo placed upon Iraq seemed to be working. It is now known that even the chief of the U.S. armed forces, General Colin Powell, advised President Bush to continue economic sanctions rather than taking military action. The need to eradicate the sense of shame, combined with an arsenal of sophisticated weapons begging to be tested in combat, made waging war too great a temptation to resist. The enemy had to be destroyed, and we had to do it.

Saddam Hussein became the perfect object upon which to unload our nearly twenty years of shame. Our president compared him to Adolf

Hitler, painting him as the most evil and ruthless despot since the Führer himself. Our shame had to become Saddam's shame. Total military victory over a despicable enemy became the only way our shame could be alleviated.

Victory Celebrations. Men and women who risk their lives for their country deserve gratitude and homecoming celebrations. But the great Desert Storm "homecoming" parades, featuring movie stars in Hollywood, parades of weapons in Washington, D.C., and over four million spectators in New York City, were not primarily homecoming celebrations. They were celebrations of victory.

There were victorious chants at each parade: "We're number one! We're number one! We're number one!" If the celebrations were simply to welcome the veterans home, then why had Vietnam vets endured such a different reception?

Military personnel in Desert Storm endured boring months in the desert under harsh conditions; they were deprived of a normal life with loved ones back home. Although fewer than two hundred American lives were lost, many soldiers were placed in life-threatening situations during combat. But the hardships and dangers faced by these men and women pale in relation to the misery Americans experienced in the jungles of Vietnam, where thousands of American lives were lost.

Obviously, the degree of hardship and sacrifice doesn't explain the difference in the two homecomings. Listen to the veterans of the Vietnam War, and you will sense the anger they still feel about the jeers and taunts they endured upon their return. They took the brunt of our shame—a shame that is misplaced, because it originates from a perverted equation: loss equals worthlessness. The inversion of this perverted notion is seen in our response to Desert Storm: masculine honor was based on the ease with which we blasted and killed more than 100,000 of the enemy.

Teaching our sons. At the heart of America's misplaced sense of identity is a warped vision of manhood. While much of the material infrastructure in the United States is in decay—deferred building and neglectful maintenance of local, state and national parks, streets and highways, water systems, waste disposal systems, schools, prisons and housing—we find a great sense of accomplishment in building weapons that allow us to be number one in war.

There is a sickness in the masculine soul of America. We've come to derive self-worth from demonstrated military power rather than from building for peace. In a spirit of repentance American fathers might do well to repeat to their sons and daughters the words of David:

My son, I had planned to build a house to the name of the Lord my God. But the word of the Lord came to me, saying: "You have shed much blood and have waged great wars; you shall not build a house to my name, because you have shed so much blood in my sight on the earth. See, a son shall be born to you; he shall be a man of peace. I will give him peace from all his enemies on every side; for his name shall be Solomon, and I will give peace and quiet to Israel in his days. He shall build a house for my name." (1 Chron 22:7-10)

Needed: The Man of Peace

Nearly all the important peacemaking positions in the world are held by men. Given the predisposition to aggression of men in every nation, how realistic is it to expect peace?

Leaders of the world's superpowers have tried to negotiate from a position of strength and superiority; both sides have put up a façade of coolness and toughness. Former President Lyndon Johnson told how he stared his opponents squarely in the eye, forcing them to be the first to turn their eyes away; thus he proved his superior position. Until recently, modern diplomacy differed little from the methods of the old gunfighter in the West, as can be seen in John Eisenhower's account of his father: "The Soviets were fully aware of Ike's Abilene heritage and the influence of the Old West on his character. When Dad said, 'you step across the line in Berlin and I'll shoot,' I think Khrushchev listened because of his background out here in 'Wild Bill Hickok' country" (Neal 1978:408). In his memoirs, dictated near the end of his life, Khrushchev said that he always admired Eisenhower for his modesty, his common sense and his many years of experience.

In the past both sides approached the peace table with their arsenals full and made little headway toward peace. The economic and political collapse of one of the superpowers has brought an opportunity to work for peace on a different basis.

In chapter four I suggested that a model of Christian manhood can be found in the person of Jesus Christ. Perhaps more than any other quality of Jesus, men today need to come to grips with the quality that caused others to refer to him as "the man of peace." We construct elaborate justifications for taking a hostile stand toward those we perceive as our enemies. But Jesus said, "Love your enemies, do good to those who hate you, bless those who curse you, pray for those who abuse you" (Lk 6:27-28); he also told Peter to forgive his brother seventy-seven times (Mt 18:22). Paul continued Jesus' teaching on what our stance should be toward our enemies: "Bless those who persecute you. . . . Do not repay anyone evil for evil. . . . If your enemies are hungry, feed them. . . . Overcome evil with good" (Rom 12:14-21).

Jesus earned the title "man of peace" by the life he lived and the words he spoke. But the apostle Paul goes beyond this title in Ephesians 2:14: "He himself is our peace; in his flesh he has made both groups into one and has broken down the dividing wall, that is, the hostility between us." Donald Kraybill (1982:176) points out,

> In context, this peace is more than just the peace of God in the believer's heart. It refers specifically to the bitter relations between Jews and Gentiles. Jesus' death didn't mysteriously extinguish Jew-Gentile hatred. Rather, it meant that both Jews and Gentiles who accepted God's forgiveness in Christ could begin loving and forgiving each other. As Jews and Gentiles repented of their sins and fellowshipped with God, the Holy Spirit empowered them to forgive even their enemies, thus crumbling the walls of hostility.

Christian manhood, then, must emulate Christ by loving and forgiving those whom we have been taught are our worst enemies. *As a man of peace* Jesus is our model, and *as our peace* he has given us the power to be men of peace like him.

7

MEN, POWER
AND CONTROL
From Intimidation to Empowering

Power does not corrupt. Fear corrupts, perhaps the fear of a loss of power.

JOHN STEINBECK

Power does not corrupt men; but fools, if they get into a position of power, corrupt power.

GEORGE BERNARD SHAW

I remember, as a boy, seeing the Charles Atlas ad—a cartoon strip that began as a well-built guy on a beach kicked sand on a skinny guy. Of course I identified with the skinny guy. As the story unfolded, the skinny guy was too weak to retaliate, and he endured the further humiliation of seeing his girl leave him for the muscular guy. For the following year, the skinny guy lifted weights, and by summertime he had developed a sculptured, muscular body. The last cartoon of the ad returned to the beach, where the girl left the brute and returned to the formerly skinny guy.

Early on, boys learn that real men are powerful, that a man without power is a wimp. While physical strength and athletic ability may be the most important signs of power during our early years, when we reach manhood occupational achievement and the ability to make money become our new signs of power.

One of the strongest male tendencies is the will to dominate, to be in control of not only oneself but also others. The way men wield power differs from one social situation to another. In formal organizations like businesses, schools and government agencies, men chart power in elaborate hierarchical, bureaucratic models. In informal impersonal relationships, such as in interaction with a store clerk, power is more ambiguous and perhaps less important. Yet power is also a concern in more intimate relationships, where it is not usually explicitly stated or recognized.

This chapter aims to explore how men gain power and use it to control others. I will suggest that rather than using power to control others, the biblically grounded male uses power to empower others.

Understanding Power

There is much confusion surrounding the issue of power, because it can be conceptualized in many different ways. Those who study power define it as one person's ability to influence or have an effect on another person's behavior. Rightly understood, power is actually the *capacity to influence,* not the exercise of that capacity. A person may have the potential power to influence but choose not to act on that power. Men who have real power will often not need to act in order to be influential. We need to distinguish between men who have established a position of power and influence because others trust them, and those who lack legitimate recognition from others but still try to influence.

Authority and dominance. One of the most important ways to classify power is on the basis of whether it is legitimate. Simply put, legitimate power is *authority* and illegitimate power is *dominance.* The man whose power is based on the support of others or sanctioned by society possesses authority. For example, most societies support the notion that parents have authority over their children until they are legally adults. The definition of adulthood differs from culture to culture, and even from state to state within the United States. So legitimate power is decided upon in various ways by different societal structures.

Dominance, on the other hand, is power that has not been recognized or sanctioned by others. It is taken without the approval of others. It is, therefore, illegitimate power. Some men go beyond the boundaries of legitimate power set by society. Society then revises their position of power. For example, parents not only are given the right but are indeed expected to discipline their children. But when a father breaks bones or inflicts bruises, burns and cuts on his wife or child, he has resorted to illegitimate power. If the courts and welfare systems are working properly, men who have abused power in such ways are denied the power that had previously been granted them.

The ability to influence is based upon the possession of valued resources and others' acceptance of one's power. In the absence of valued resources and legitimate norms, a person may resort to intimidation or brute force in an attempt to influence. The father who abuses his children does so because he *lacks* legitimate power. A husband who has the respect of his wife has power because of that respect. A husband who does not have the respect of his wife often resorts to verbal and physical abuse in the attempt to gain control. In reality, such men are weak and ineffective in their attempts to influence legitimately—they have no authority. Lacking authority, such men resort to illegitimate means of control—dominance.

In his book *Winning Through Intimidation* (1979), Robert Ringer claims that although one may not possess many skills and resources, one can gain power through intimidating others. His book is full of clever tricks that will enhance a man's position of power. He suggests that a man should dress in a certain manner to project a powerful image, control situations by meeting people on his own turf (his office) and purposefully make others wait a few minutes before a meeting begins, and request that his secretary buzz him during the meeting so that his guest sees how important and powerful he is. These manipulations are designed to give one the upper hand.

Ascribed and achieved power. In monarchy, all rulers, merely by being anointed or crowned, possess legitimate civil power and authority. Their civil power is based upon their *ascribed* status. Their power is not earned, but is merely possessed because they have a given status or position in society.

In other societies, rule by monarchy has been replaced by democracy. Here, the mere fact of being of royal lineage does *not* guarantee legitimate civil authority. In these societies, *resources* become an important condition for gaining civil authority. Property, money, education, knowledge, interpersonal and managerial skills and personality, if recognized and valued by the people who vote, can become the sources of civil authority. Such civil authority is based upon a person's *achieved* status. This power is not inherited through birth into a prestigious family. Individuals born into a prestigious family do have access to resources, but they can gain power only if these resources are valued by the citizens.

In family life, men in traditional societies usually hold power over women because power is ascribed to the *male* who occupies the position of family head. In modern urban societies, however, family positions and power are much more likely to be based upon achieved status. Currently, most power is earned by individuals' behaving in ways that are valued, respected and trusted by others.

Obviously, there are positions of power in any society that are still inherited or ascribed, but people in these positions must prove their worth over the long haul in order to keep their power. A major source of conflict in some families is that men and women use a different basis for assessing power. Men who need to control hold to an ascribed power system, while women who resent being controlled will opt for a system in which power is based on achievement.

Orchestrative and implementative power. Another way of conceptualizing power is to distinguish between *orchestrative* power and *implementative* power. To possess orchestrative power is to be in a position where one can delegate power to another. To have implementative power is to have the power to make decisions because it has been delegated by the one who has orchestrative power.

In marital systems in which the husband is expected to function as the head of the home, it's often the wife who actually wields most of the power and makes the important decisions regarding the family. An outsider may conclude that she has most of the family power (influence), which, indeed, may be the case. But she may simply have implementative power, delegated to her by her husband. In reality, the family still sees him as the primary center of power.

In a sense, there's an inverse relationship between how powerful one is and how active one must be in order to be influential. A really powerful person can be influential without trying to be, and a less powerful person may have to work very hard to be influential. A very powerful father needs to speak a request only once and his children obey, while fathers who lack power raise their voices and bark out threatening commands to try to bring about compliance.

Power must also be understood from an organizational perspective. Some organizations give a deceptive view of the seat of power by setting up figureheads who merely carry out the wishes of the powerful. Here the most powerful persons hold the orchestrative power and the figureheads hold the implementative power.

Using Power to Control Women

Crosscultural research shows that men the world over use their power to dominate women. Almost all societies can be characterized as patriarchal, where ultimate authority resides with men. But why is this so? Why do men try to control women?

One explanation is that men seek power over women simply because it is in their rational self-interest to do so. Having power over women gives men concrete benefits such as choice jobs, food and ownership of material goods, plus the most prestige and privileged status in society. The reason men have power over women rather than the other way around is explained by men's greater average physical size and strength. Although men may have originally dominated women through brute force, ideological and religious beliefs and norms were conveniently developed later to justify men's position of power over women.

Behavioral scientists have attempted to give explanations as to why men use power to control women. I will give brief summaries of four of the most popular of these explanations.[1]

Reproduction of mothering. Nancy Chodorow believes that there is a fundamental personality difference between males and females result-

---

[1]The last three of these explanations are summaries of insights I have gained from chapter sixteen of Joseph Pleck's *The American Man* (1980).

ing from the fact that most parenting is done by mothers rather than fathers. Building upon Chodorow's ideas, Carol Gilligan (1982) has found that males and females make moral decisions on a different basis. Whereas men emphasize hierarchy, rights and autonomy, women emphasize context, caring and attachment. While women are more optimistic that problems can be solved through relationships and by relying upon the process of communication, men rely on the conventions of logic and abstract rules, and they control attempts to ensure fairness.

The implication of these found gender differences is that males more than females have a psychological need to be in control in interpersonal relationships. There is a psychological barrier within males that works against mutuality in relationships, moving them instead to use power as a means of obtaining security. According to Gilligan (1982:42), "Men feel secure alone at the top of a hierarchy, securely separate from the challenge of others. Women feel secure in the middle of a web of relationships; to be at the top of a hierarchy is seen as disconnected."

Women more than men see life as dependent on connection, sustained by activities of care and based on a bond of attachment—characteristics that encourage women to use power to empower rather than to control. Men live by the injunction to respect the rights of others, and to protect the rights to life and self-fulfillment. These characteristics encourage men to use power to control. Men have a fear of being in a dependent position. This fear motivates them to grab for more power, and when they have it, to hoard it like a nonrenewable resource.

Experience of early female domination. A similar explanation is that men seek to control women as adults because as children they experienced women as oppressing them. In a society in which women are not given equal authority with men, women inadvertently will seek to control males whenever they're given a chance. The two arenas in which women do have authority are the home and the elementary classroom—and these just happen to be the places in which young boys spend much of their early childhood. In fact, most American males spend their early years moving between a female-dominated home and a female-dominated classroom.

The result is that adult men have an unconscious fear of being controlled by women. The way men handle this fear is to make sure that women are never again in a position of control over them. The best defense against being controlled is to develop a good offense; thus men seek to control women as a defense against the fear they have of being controlled by them.

Women's expressive power. According to the traditional definition of gender roles, men achieve and women give the emotional support men need as they struggle to achieve. Within such an arrangement, women can satisfy their need to achieve only vicariously, through the achievements of men. Traditionally, it was expected that when a women married she would give up any career ambitions and invest all her energies in her husband and his career.

In their preoccupation with achieving success at their jobs, men came to neglect their own emotional needs. The solution for this lack of balance was to become dependent upon women for their emotional needs. Women came to do emotional work for men—to feel for them. Men and women came to exist in a mutually dependent relationship. While women satisfied their need for achievement through their husbands, men experienced their emotions vicariously through their wives.

Men need women in order to feel emotionally alive. Men seek to control women due to their emotional need for them. With gender roles now in flux, men fear that if they lose control over women, they will no longer be able to get their emotional needs met.

Women's masculinity-validating power. In societies that sharply distinguish between male and female roles, each gender depends upon the other for gender-role validation. The traditional female is to be soft, pretty, gentle and nice to look at. Women develop a need to be noticed and admired in terms of these characteristics. Masculinity carries with it the expectation that men are strong, independent, reliable and sexually potent. This places both women and men in the position of being dependent upon the other to have their femininity and masculinity validated. A man actually needs to be near a woman who will assure him that he is strong. Even when a men is less than capable, a supportive woman will affirm, "Oh honey, you are so strong, I just don't know how I could manage without you."

The problem for men, then, comes when women become strong, independent and reliable themselves. Now they no longer need to look to a man to be strong for them. The obvious loss for the man is that the woman no longer validates his masculine power. What many men fear in the women's movement is a potential loss in women's masculinity-validating power. So fearful men will try to maintain the mechanism of control over women.

Alternative Uses of Power

I have proposed that power is simply the ability to influence another. There are, however, a number of different ways in which men can try to influence others. Rollo May, in his book *Love and Will* (1969), identifies five types of power: *exploitative*, or influencing by brute force; *manipulative*, or influencing by devious social psychological means; *competitive*, influencing based upon the possession of resources; *nutritive*, such as in parent-child relationships, where power eventually outlives its usefulness; and *integrative*, in which one person uses power for another's sake.

Due to the larger average size of men and the superordinate position usually assigned to them, men are more apt than women to utilize exploitation and competition. These are both attempts to influence based on a model of hedonistic self-interest. Men's greater participation in the marketplace, where the values of individualism, competition and materialism are stressed, make them more prone to adopt hedonistic self-interest. Because of their greater involvement in the home and parenting, women are more apt to utilize a nutritive model of influencing others. Since women are usually assigned the subordinate position, they are also more apt to resort to manipulation.

In their attempts to influence the behavior of others, men are also noted for their *paternalism*. Although paternalism includes elements of nutritive power, it also carries the connotation that men will do what is best for others because of their superior position, wisdom, knowledge or skills. The paternalistic model of power is still very much present in contemporary society. In the traditional family model, for instance, power is assumed to reside with the husband because of the position he occupies. Ideological justifications that attempt to go beyond mere cultural tradition usually defend the patriarchal model as the way God intended power issues to be handled in the family. The man has been placed in the position of headship for the sake of resolving issues of disagreement in the family.

In some of the extreme versions of the traditional patriarchal family, the husband has dictatorial rule, ordering his wife and children around as he sees fit. In other versions that have been tempered with Christianity, his rule is usually more of a benevolent dictatorship. In the most authoritarian Christian version, the father is placed just below God in a chain of command that extends downward to the mother and then the child. The father is in an absolute power position over his wife and children. Children are to submit to both father and mother, the wife is to submit to her husband and the husband is to submit to God. Noticeably absent is the concept of mutual submission or the suffering servant model of Philippians 2:1-11.

In less authoritarian Christian versions of the patriarchal model, the husband is seen as head of his wife as Christ was head of the church—in the role of a suffering servant. The father/husband remains head of the home, however, and he is expected to assume the responsibility and decision-making power that goes along with this position.

Erich Fromm (1956) has observed that socializing children is the process of getting the children to want to do what they have to do. From this perspective, the socialization of children can be described in both nutritive and paternalistic terms. Within a nutritive model, however, external control (the wishes of the more powerful) is transferred into internal control (the child's wanting to do what is desired by the other). In a paternalistic model there is generally not a transfer of control. When control is not given up, there is a perpetuation of *dependency*.

When power is truly used for another's sake—the power that May calls *integrative*—there will be a giving up of control. This, I believe, is the *empowering* model presented in Scripture.

Empowering: The Biblical Model

Investigations on men's use of power—and the social science models that have been developed—have assumed that men will attempt to increase their own power and decrease that of others. While I don't deny that most men's use of power can probably be analyzed on the basis of this assumption, I also think a universal application of such an assumption causes one to overlook what I believe is the biblical model of the use of power—*empowering.*

The concept of empowering has to do with the *use* of power. One way of describing empowering is that it is an attempt to develop power in another person. But empowering is not merely yielding to the wishes of another person. Nor does it necessarily involve giving up one's own power to someone else. Rather, empowering is the active and intentional process of developing power within another person. The person who is empowered has gained power because of the empowering behavior of the other. It is an interactive process between two people.

Nutritive power may or may not be a good example of empowering, depending on motives. What May calls integrative power, however, is a clear example of empowering. May cites Jesus as an example of a person who used integrative power. In stating his central message, Jesus said, "I came that they may have life, and have it abundantly" (Jn 10:10). May sees Gandhi's nonviolent resistance as an attempt to use power to empower not only the oppressed but the oppressor as well. Empowering seeks to strengthen and heal weak, broken or dependent relationships.

Empowering and limited-supply theory. The concept of empowering makes no sense if power is perceived to be in limited supply. Most attempts to analyze men's use of power are based upon a limited-supply assumption. The social exchange perspective, for example, assumes that there are a maximum number of power units available in any relationship. In marriage, for example, power may be represented as one hundred units to be divided up between the husband and wife. The husband may have all the power (one hundred units) and the wife none (zero units); the wife may have slightly more power (sixty units) than the husband (forty units); or (in the egalitarian marriage) fifty units may be allocated to each spouse. Scott Bartchy (1984) points out that within a limited-supply view of power, one spouse must control at least fifty-one power units to be in a position of control. This is obviously an inadequate way to promote the empowering process.

The message of the Bible is that the power of God is available to all men (and women) in *unlimited* amounts. In social relationships, the one who empowers will benefit and be empowered in the very action of empowering. Empowered persons are in a relationship of mutual and reciprocal empowering. Therefore, as each person's power increases, there is more potential for further empowering—not a decrease in personal power.

Structural barriers. If a comparative study of human societies teaches us anything, it is that men use power as a means to suppress and control others. The most effective social uses of power for suppression and control are found in institutional structures. Some would suggest that human history can best be understood in terms of three systems of human domination—class, race/ethnicity and sex/gender (Ferguson 1984).

As the dominant group begins to use power, *reification* takes place, meaning that the justification of the powerful comes to be a part of social ideology. The subordinate group is no longer considered to be oppressed, but rather subject to the rule of the more powerful because of inequality in abilities.

Any attempt at building a just society must deal with the problem of inequality and power. It is noteworthy that two of the persons who have given the modern world utopian ideologies, Jesus Christ and Karl Marx, both incorporate the practice of empowering into their image of an ideal society.

Although Marx has been proclaimed by many to be the enemy of Jesus, it is noteworthy that like Jesus, Marx found it necessary to radically alter the conventional definition and use of power. He rightly pointed out that where there are inequalities of access to valued resources, the result will be abuse of power—for as I stated earlier, resources are the modern basis for power. Marx's solution is amazingly similar to that of the early Christians: owning all things in common and giving to each according to their needs.

The problem with Marx's solution is that he believed evil to be in-

herent in certain types of economic social structures, rather than eman-
ating from the hearts of human beings. Communism is an ideal system
for saints. The problem is that we are all sinners, and we need a system
that will hold us accountable for our self-centeredness. We need to
recognize that both unequal access to valued resources and lack of
accountability are structural barriers to empowering.

The example of Jesus. What Jesus taught about power was so central
to his mission that it became the basis for all human relationships. Jesus'
view of power can be seen in his response to James and John's request,
"Grant us to sit, one at your right hand and one at your left, in your
glory" (Mk 10:37). Having shared Jesus' earthly ministry, they wanted
to rule with him as well—to be the extension of the power he would
have when he reigned. But Jesus denied their request:

> You know that among the Gentiles those whom they recognize as
> their rulers lord it over them, and their great ones are tyrants over
> them. But it is not so among you; but whoever wants to become great
> among you must be your servant, and whoever wants to be first among
> you must be slave of all. For the Son of Man came not to be served
> but to serve, and to give his life a ransom for many. (Mk 10:42-45)

We first need to note Jesus' disapproval of persons' using their power
to "lord it over" others. According to Jesus, power is to be used *for
others*; one who has power is to be a "servant" or "slave of all." That
this is to be the normative way in which all Christians are to use power
is confirmed by Jesus' example: he tells his disciples that "the Son of
Man came not to be served but to serve."

Jesus redefined power by his teachings and life. He rejected the use
of power to control others; instead, he affirmed the use of power to
serve others, to lift up the fallen, to forgive, to encourage responsibility
and maturity and to give power to the powerless.

The relationship of Jesus to his disciples can be understood only in
terms of the empowering theme. Preparing his disciples for his departure, Jesus promised that the Holy Spirit would be present as comforter
and helper to help them accomplish their ministry (Jn 16). Later, in Acts
1:8, he assures them, "But you will receive power when the Holy Spirit
comes on you."

It's good to ponder the type of community these disciples developed after Jesus' ascension. Acts 2:44-45 says, "All who believed were together and had all things in common; they would sell their possessions and goods and distribute the proceeds to all, as any had need." The logical end result of Jesus' teaching was servanthood; his followers gave up to each other the very resources upon which conventional power is based.

Jesus modeled a power of strength for serving, rather than controlling, others. Christian manhood involves using power *for* others. It means we must resist our natural tendency to use power to control others and to serve ourselves. In the hands of a true Christian warrior, power will be used for the benefit of others—and the power will spread.

8

MALE SEXUALITY
Releasing the Lover

When we who are male think of sexuality, we usually think of "sex," and that means genital experience. We do not think first, or primarily, of sensuousness or of an emotionally intimate relationship, though these often enter in at some later point. Rather, our focus is more on sexual acts, acts involving genital expression. In turn, we tend to isolate sex from other areas of life.

JAMES NELSON, *THE INTIMATE CONNECTION*

A 1991 article on sexual impotence in *U.S. News & World Report* opened with the comment: "You can tell your best friend you have cancer, and the agony of facing loss of life is eased somewhat in the sharing. But who can you tell that you've lost your manhood?" The obvious point is that men define their manhood in terms of their capacity to perform sexually.

A few years ago, I was conducting research on men's attitudes toward vasectomy as a means of birth control. I found that the most common reasons men gave for not considering a vasectomy had to do with concern for how it might affect their manhood. They said, "No way, I'm not going to have my manhood taken away from me," and "I would be less of a man if I didn't have the capacity to produce children." To be a man is to be sexually potent.

The Development of Male Sexuality
Our sexual identity is a complex part of ourselves, difficult to fathom. While our sexuality was designed by God, it also is tainted by our

fallenness. While there is a strong physiological and biological component to our sexuality, it is also formed and shaped by social and cultural factors. How and what we are taught about sex are powerful forces in shaping our attitudes toward our sexuality. The making of male sexuality involves the interplay of a number of factors.

Sociocultural roots. Sociocultural factors are extremely important in shaping male sexuality. As an example, men are generally regarded as being more sexual than females. But the evidence seems to indicate that, if in fact this is true, it is largely due to the greater cultural restraints placed on the expression of sexuality among females. As little girls grow up, parents take a more sexually protective stance toward them. Girls are warned to be modest in the way they dress and to guard themselves against boys' sexual advances. The message boys receive is generally much less restrictive. Boys are given more freedom to uncover their bodies and explore themselves physically.

As boys grow into puberty, they become part of adolescent male subcultures where they are encouraged to make sexual overtures toward girls as a sign of their masculinity. The message that male sexuality is expressed in aggressiveness is reflected in the language of the subculture. Boys describe "successful" sexual encounters with girls in terms of "scoring" or "making it." The boy who fails to "score" is in danger of having his sexuality called into question.

By the time they reach adulthood, males have been culturally conditioned to be sexually active, while females have been conditioned to resist sexual stimuli and sexual advances.

What males find sexually arousing is also largely determined by culture. While small breasts were part of the feminine ideal in the past, males today are much more likely to be turned on by large breasts. What men find sexually stimulating in one culture may carry no erotic meaning in another. In my youth I heard a female missionary tell of her first term experience on the mission field in an African country. As she walked through a rural village for the first time, the men whistled at her. Surprised, she asked a more experienced missionary to explain this enthusiastic reception. It seems that men in this particular culture were sexually attracted to women with plump legs.

The extent to which male sexual responsiveness is culturally conditioned is also suggested through the changes in women's bathing suits over the last one hundred years. During Victorian times, men and women were not even permitted to bathe together on a public beach. When mixed bathing came to be more culturally acceptable (around the turn of the century), bathing suits were made to cover the woman's body all the way down to her ankles and wrists. As cultural norms have changed throughout the twentieth century, women have been encouraged to expose more of their bodies. This increasing exposure has diminished the sexual stimulus of various body parts. While a bare knee would have caused quite a stir around the turn of the century, it is not the focus of erotic attention today.

Suppose that a young man living at the turn of the century could be placed in a time capsule and transported to a typical beach in the United States today. Conditioned by the modesty of dress and sexual conventions of the 1890s, he would be totally shocked, to say the least! Clearly, men's sexual responses are largely determined by social and cultural conditioning.

Sex is a strong human urge, and every society finds ways to curtail sexuality. The way sexuality is curtailed or allowed to find free expression greatly affects male sexuality. For example, compare the attempts to control sex during the Victorian era with practices in traditional Muslim societies. While the Victorians' strategy was to repress sex itself, the strategy in Muslim societies is also specifically designed to repress women.

The Victorians expended enormous energy attempting to curtail and repress sexual passion in males. Women's clothes were designed to hide most parts of their bodies. Even though women's bathing suits were extremely modest, mixed bathing was prohibited just to make sure men would be spared sexual temptation. And not only were women expected to cover their arms and legs in public, but even the legs of the living-room sofa and chairs were covered with little skirts. Bare legs on furniture were considered a symbol of sexual immodesty.

An article in one of the leading magazines in 1870, *Nation*, advised that "the sexual passion—the animal, brute passion, through which

God, apparently in the ignorance of 'moral progress,' has provided for the perpetuation of the human species is the most untameable of all the passions, and is an inseparable concomitant of physical health, and though susceptible of control by moral means, is not capable of extinction or repression."

In Muslim societies all public space is declared "male space"—off limits to a woman unless she is escorted by a man. Women themselves are veiled, not so much to protect them as to protect men from female sexuality. For women, because they are women, are thought to have a natural advantage over men. If not suppressed, women's sexuality would cause *fitna*, or chaos, in society; men would be defenseless before the dangers of female sexuality.

Sexual Desire and Love

The Victorians also drew a sharp line between sexual desire and love. Men were taught that it was virtuous to marry a woman for whom they had pure thoughts—which meant no sexual desire. Husbands were told that if they really loved their wives, they would try to abstain from having sex with them too often, for even in marriage, sexual relationships were considered to be degrading to women.

The expert medical opinion of the day was that any sexual desire in a young woman was pathological. In 1867, the Surgeon General of the United States proclaimed that nine-tenths of the time, "decent" women did not feel the "slightest pleasure" in sexual intercourse. The Ann Landers columnist of the day, John Cowan, wrote this wisdom in his advice column: "The more a woman yields to the demands of animal passion in her husband, the more he loses his love and respect for her."

And what should any upright male do who began to feel sexual attraction for a woman? He should look squarely into her eyes and imagine that he saw the face of his *mother*. In a newspaper column in 1878, young men were given this advice about mate selection: "Every son, 'Behold thy mother.' Make love to her, and her your first sweetheart. Be courteous, gallant, and her knight-errant, and your nearest friend and bosom confidant. Nestle yourself right into her heart, and her into yours. Seek her 'company' and advice, and imbibe her purifying influences.

Learn how to court by courting her." It's not coincidental that one of the most popular songs at the turn of the century contained the line, "I want a girl just like the girl who married dear old Dad."

The relationship between mothers and sons during the late 1800s was a very emotional, almost erotic, attachment. The wisdom of the day assumed that it would be the mother rather than the father who instructed male children about sexual behavior and morality. Mothers had a hard time giving their sons up to marriage—and it became even harder as the sons got older. Interestingly, most of the psychological theories developed in the late 1800s were dominated by mother-son relationship concerns.

The sexual desire/love dichotomy of the Victorian era led to the double standard in which men had their sexual needs met by the "bad" woman but would marry only the "good" woman. This perversion within the male sexual psyche continues even to this day. Men are still psychologically bound by a sexual script that calls them to be respectfully nonsexual toward the women they love and erotically free with "bad" women. A tragic example of this is Jimmy Swaggart's taking a prostitute to a seedy motel room, leaving his strikingly beautiful wife at home. Sex therapists note that many men can become sexually aroused with their wives only by fantasizing that they are making love to a slut or a whore. Feelings of tenderness and high esteem toward the wife lead to a deflation of sexual desire, while feelings of degradation and debasement release the male's erotic feelings.

The residue of the sexual desire/love dichotomy can be seen in a diverse range of contemporary mass media depictions of male sexuality—in advertising, magazines, literature, music videos and films. The image of male sexuality depicted in *Playboy* magazine or any of its many imitators bears this out. *Playboy* found an eager audience among young males who were ready to embrace the view that sex is meant to be enjoyed free from the encumbrances of love and commitment. Denying the complex richness of womanhood, the playboy philosophy reduces woman to a single dimension, making her a sex object. *Playboy* had great appeal to insecure males who were terrified at the thought of relating to a multidimensional woman.

According to the playboy philosophy, any red-blooded American male must learn to be a skilled manipulator of women, able to "score" in bed. Such men will know when to turn the lights down, what music to play on the stereo, which drinks to serve and how to steer the conversation. The playboy reduces sexuality to a consumer item that he can handle because it demands no responsibility. It is sex devoid of love. The bed is shared, but the playboy emerges free of any emotional attachment or commitment. When playtime is over, the plaything can be discarded in a manner befitting our use-and-throw-away society. If the young man happened to lose his heart to a woman, the Great Bunny in the Sky would be quick to condemn him: "You goofed!"

The James Bond films exemplify the dichotomization of sexual desire and love. In each of these films, Bond interacts with women with a cool air of detachment. Women fall passionately in love with him, but he remains above it all. In one noteworthy scene, Bond is embarrassing a woman while he prepares to give her a kiss. Kissing her, he sees a reflection in her eye: a man is sneaking up behind him with a knife. As the man lunges forward, Bond whirls the woman around, so that the knife plunges into her back rather than his. I should add that the woman was a double agent who was setting Bond up to be killed.

In one James Bond film, Bond actually falls in love, and we see the two wed in a stylish church high in the Alps. But Ian Fleming, the author of the James Bond novels, hides a message for men in this episode. As Bond and his bride drive away to begin their honeymoon, they are chased by enemies, and following a volley of gunshots Bond's bride of thirty minutes is killed. For the first time in his life Bond experiences grief: the one woman he has loved is taken from him. Fleming's message to men is poignant and disturbing: Men can be emotionally safe only by separating sex from love; if a man loses his heart to a woman, he runs the risk of experiencing grief.

A Sexually Saturated Society

In the 1950s and 1960s our society was *preoccupied* with sex. This preoccupation began with the publication of the "Kinsey reports"— *Sexual Behavior in the Human Male* (1948) and *Sexual Behavior in the*

Human Female (1952). These were quickly followed by the launching of *Playboy* magazine. In it Hugh Hefner proclaimed himself a modern-day Moses and promised to lead us out of the wilderness of sexual bondage into the land of sexual freedom. Our society's preoccupation with sex ended with the demise of the hippie movement, which sought to challenge uptight sexual attitudes and celebrated sexual freedom.

Writing about this period, C. S. Lewis gives a hypothetical illustration of a society in which people paid good money to enter a room to view a covered platter sitting on a table. At the assigned time and to the flourish of drums, someone would very slowly lift the cover and expose the object that had been hidden. To everyone's surprise, what was revealed was a *pork chop*! Lewis goes on to surmise that one would begin to wonder what was wrong with the eating habits of the people in such a society.

The point is well taken. We do well to ask that same question of our sexually preoccupied society, "What are we to make of its sexual habits?"

Since the 1960s, American society has actually gone a step further: the platter is no longer covered. We have become *saturated* with sex. Sex is front-page news. It is openly explored in the words of popular music and in music videos; sex is the "hook" advertisements use to gain our attention, and we are served graphic sexual encounters in the movies and on the afternoon soap operas.

In the 1950s, television programs could not even show a married couple in the same bed. Remember Ozzie and Harriet saying good night to each other from their twin beds? To see the slightest cleavage of a woman's breasts one had to go the movies.

In the past thirty years the depiction of sexual behavior has progressively gotten more explicit. What might have been thought of as risqué in the 1950s would probably not even garner a "PG" movie rating today. As the depiction of sex in the media has become more and more explicit, the principle of diminishing returns has been in effect. Once the public becomes saturated with a certain degree of sexual explicitness, the media must depict sex *more* explicitly in order to elicit the same response. Things are such today that the line about Kansas City in the musical *Oklahoma* seems appropriate—"they've gone about as far as they can go."

Men who have adopted the playboy philosophy of sexual freedom may be suffering from diminishing returns as well. They have experienced sex with a variety of partners, in a variety of ways, under a variety of conditions. When sex for the sake of sex is the goal, an ever-heightened stimulus is needed in order for men to achieve erotic excitement. One of the grosser examples of this is the recent report that a well-known Hollywood movie star was rushed to the hospital to have a live gerbil removed from his rectum. Men whose lives have been saturated with sex will become almost frantic in their efforts to verify that they are still sexually potent.

How many males must have harbored a secret envy of Hugh Hefner as he fulfilled his sexual desires with a never-ending series of young, generously endowed Playmates-of-the-Month? Who could ask for anything more? And yet we shouldn't have been all that surprised that after nearly forty years of living out the playboy philosophy, he decided to marry again. Could it be that for the playboy of the Western world sex had ceased to bring any real returns at all? Perhaps his only hope was to find sex and love in the same woman.

Sex and Power

The expectation that males must be competitive, aggressive and achievement-oriented carries over into sexual activities. We are currently being shocked to learn of the prevalence of date rape—rape that takes place in a dating situation. One study found that twenty-five per cent of men had tried to have sexual intercourse with a woman against her wishes. Another reported that twenty-five per cent of women had experienced their first sexual intercourse under force or a sense of obligation.

The male sexuality we have inherited defines itself in the will to conquer, dominate and control. Male sexuality is integrally bound up with power.

The relationship between male sexuality and power may have to do with the nature of sexual barter between males and females. Our sexual scripts call for males to attempt to go as far as they can sexually; it is up to the female to set the limits. The person who shows less interest in a sexual encounter assumes the more powerful position. Power in a relationship is the ability to control the resources. Males define sexual access to the female as a desired resource much more than females define access to males as a resource. This means that females are expected to control the level of sexual involvement.

So males are left in the position of trying to overcome females' perceived power. When it comes to sexual involvement, women are in the more powerful position. Some men, especially those who feel that they are powerless to gain access to sex, resort to dominance and force.

While not all men are consumers of pornography, it is possible to learn something of the sexual psyches of men by noting recurring themes in pornography. Male dominance over women is the major theme in pornographic literature the world over. In fact, the Greek root *pornia* means "female captives." Pornography is nearly exclusively consumed by males. The core themes in pornography are subjugation, aggression, degradation, abuse, coercion, violence, dominance, control, sadism and rape. This is exemplified in the classic French erotic novel *O,* about a secret society in which all females must be submissive and sexually accessible to all males. Erotic arousal in the male mind seems to be greatly facilitated by images of men's power over women.

In its most perverted form, the male equation of sex and power expresses itself in the physical abuse of women. Sexual violence is nearly always committed by males. Sexually violent acts, such as rape, are attempts to fulfill nonsexual needs. The typical rapist is a weak person with extremely low self-esteem; he feels powerless and ineffectual in his relationships with both males and females. Most rapists report that the assault did not provide sexual satisfaction or pleasure. Rape is primarily a violent act in which the perpetrator attempts to deal with his aggression and desire for power.

While only a small minority of men commit sexual violence, research on the effects of pornography on the attitudes and beliefs of random samples of men is truly scary. One study found that after viewing pornography, forty-one per cent of a group of university males reported that they might rape if they were certain of not being caught. It seems that male sexuality reflects a sexist culture that includes unequal power between men and women, dehumanization of sex and degradation of women.

Authentic Male Sexuality

It is tempting to begin a search for authentic male sexuality by seeking to understand how men are to *behave* sexually. Achieving authentic male sexuality, however, depends more on understanding who God created men to *be* as sexual persons. How men behave sexually certainly influences how we define ourselves as sexual beings, and vice versa. But understanding what it means to be created as a sexual male in God's image involves much more than a simple assent to, or an ability to live up to, particular behavioral standards.

To begin with, I repeat that although God created our sexuality, it bears the taint of our fallen nature. I've shown that much that is inauthentic about male sexuality reflects a corrupt culture. Now I will attempt to distinguish authentic from inauthentic male sexuality in three areas—autoeroticism, homosexuality and marital sexuality.

Autoeroticism. Autoeroticism is self-generated sexual activity directed toward oneself. From an early age, boys engage in more autoeroticism than girls. The reason for this is probably that it is easier for boys to discover their penises than for girls to discover their sexual responsiveness. The greater sexual self-stimulation among males than females is true for persons at all ages. Studies find that nearly all males masturbate, with Kinsey finding that ninety-six per cent of males report masturbating to orgasm.

Not long ago, a number of consequences were fabricated in an attempt to discourage boys from masturbating. Folk wisdom claimed such punishments as hair falling out; breaking out in warts, pimples or a skin disease; going blind; becoming impotent; and so on. Perhaps only a few men can remember growing up with the fear of these physical manifestations, but many of us have experienced intense guilt about masturbation.

How should we view masturbation, and what should we teach our sons? Obviously, those of us who are fathers should alleviate the fears and guilt that myths of the past may have perpetuated. It's very natural for boys to explore their bodies. They need to feel affirmed about their bodies and their good feelings when they touch themselves. It is also important that boys sense a freedom about nudity and comfort with their fathers' reactions to their bodies and their sexual responses.

The Bible is completely silent on the topic of masturbation. Any scriptural case a person builds, either for or against masturbation, must be based on inferences. I've come across three major opinions about the place of masturbation in a Christian's life. The most *restrictive* position is that masturbation, under any circumstance, is sinful. The most *permissive* position holds that masturbation under any circumstance is healthy and morally permissible. This position considers masturbation as harmful to no one and a good way to be aware of and responsive to ourselves as sexual beings. A more *moderate* view holds that masturbation can be healthy and morally appropriate, but that it has the potential to be unhealthy and morally inappropriate as well.

To me, the moderate position seems to be the most reasonable. Masturbation can be a healthy, enjoyable way for a man without a marital partner to experience sexual gratification. God has created humans as sexual beings, and autoeroticism can help people be aware of and in touch with their sexuality. Many Christian men need to be released from the guilty feelings they have about masturbation and taught to thank God for the affirmation of their sexuality.

But masturbation is not always psychologically and morally healthy. Compulsive masturbation, like compulsive eating and compulsive sleeping, can be harmful. Many males become plagued with sexual addictions that gain control over them and become destructive. Masturbation can also be used as an escape from frustration. Studies have shown that masturbation greatly increases among college males in the last weeks of the semester; they use masturbation to reduce anxiety and escape the unpleasant tasks of writing term papers and studying for final exams. Such sexual release should be regarded as possibly harmful and disruptive, but not sinful.

Masturbation within marriage is unhealthy when it deprives one's wife of sexual fulfillment. Married men who resort to masturbation may be choosing erotic isolation and disconnectedness. If a couple is unwilling to work on sexual problems in the marriage relationship and they resort to masturbation rather than seeking counseling, both the relationship and the individual partners may be harmed. The relationship must always have priority, and the couple needs to face sexual problems—and any other marital problems—rather than escaping them.

Another issue to contemplate is the connection between masturbation and lust. Jesus addresses this in Matthew 5:27-28: "You have heard that it was said, 'You shall not commit adultery.' But I say to you that everyone who looks at a woman with lust has already committed adultery with her in his heart." Jesus describes a situation in which a man is lusting after a specific woman. Lusting after a particular person may lead one to act out that lust by actually taking another person's spouse. This is adultery and adultery is sin.

But lusting should not necessarily be equated with fantasizing. Most men fantasize about future possibilities, and it may be that masturbating as one envisions one's spouse or future spouse could be a helpful practice. Lusting has to do with wanting something very intensely and seeking ways to fulfill that desire. Fantasy, on the other hand, occurs when one wishes for something in a general sense, and the one fantasizing does not usually attempt to achieve that exact fantasy. The person who is fantasizing can usually tell the difference.

If a man's fantasies turn into lusting for the object of the fantasy, that's another matter. The pedophile, for example, may masturbate and fantasize about having sex with young children, then lust for and find a young victim with whom to act out the fantasy. Obviously this is a sinful act, and the fantasy was a precursor to acting out that sin. Men should pay attention to their fantasies and be willing to keep them within God's purposes.

As an example, a man may fantasize about destroying or defeating another person because he wants power. Bringing such a fantasy to awareness makes it possible to consider whether this is God's intended purpose. This fantasy disregards God's commandments to love others and not do them harm. In the same way, men who view erotic pictures while masturbating may want to consider the moral question of sexual exploitation and the dehumanizing aspects of the erotic material to judge whether this practice is in keeping with God's intention for them. The major concern about pornography has to do with these issues, for harmful and distorted attitudes and beliefs about women and sex in our culture may lead to an increase in rape and other crimes against them. Again, the Bible admonishes us to cherish and value one another, not to degrade and devalue others.

Christian men must consider these sorts of questions in trying to work out what one is free to do and what is good to do. Each of us must determine the appropriateness of his own fantasies and check the effect they have on his whole life and what he believes about God's creation. It's possible to monitor our thoughts, just as it's possible to choose what we allow to influence our thoughts about world affairs, attitudes toward the poor and many other beliefs.

The married man who is drawn to a romantic fantasy needs to consider whether it takes away from his marriage or increases his responsiveness and receptiveness to his spouse. The single male needs to decide whether the fantasy kindles his hope in a future relationship according to God's plan, or whether the idealism of his fantasy makes him less likely to love a real live person who won't live up to the fantasy. Overall, the principle is that when what we fantasize is not in keeping with God's intention for created wholeness, we need to recognize this and change our thoughts, bringing them in line with God's plan for our full sexual manhood.

Homosexuality. Although most men have a sexual preference for women, it is estimated that approximately one out of every twenty men in the United States has a sexual preference for men.

A simple definition of homosexuality is "sexual attraction and orientation toward members of the same sex." Most adult homosexuals report that when they were younger they sensed that they were "different" from their peers, and that they struggled for years with issues of gender-role nonconformity. Adolescence can be an especially painful time for homosexuals, because like other boys they have a great fear of being different; they are often cruelly labeled "queer" by their peers. The gay identity develops over considerable time through a process of discovery.

Most homosexuals have gone through a period of hiding their identity, living in great fear of being discovered. This is a realistic fear, because many people in our society feel free to express great hatred and contempt of homosexual men. Homophobia may be defined as excessive or compulsive hatred or fear of homosexuals. Homophobic reactions in men often stem from an insecurity about their own sexuality, but can be the result of ignorance about homosexuality and homosexuals. It is important for Christian men to understand the great pain many homosexuals have faced in our homophobic society, and to offer our friendship, compassion and acceptance to our homosexual brothers.

Homosexuality, at least in part, may have a biological base. Where biological factors are important, they probably contribute to general tendencies rather than determining sexual preference. Bell, Weinberg and Hammersmith (1981:216) report that the origins of heterosexuality or homosexuality cannot be firmly established, but they state that biological factors "are not inconsistent with what one would expect to find if, indeed, there were a biological basis for sexual preference." If there is a biological precursor, it is most certainly combined with certain cultural factors.

Homosexuality has existed with varying acceptance in most societies throughout history. Most attempts to explain homosexuality refer to sociocultural factors. The most popular explanation of homosexuality in the twentieth century has come from psychoanalytic theory. According to this theory, the origin of same-sex preference is an aberrant psychosexual development during the "genital stage," when children are working through the Oedipal and Electra complexes. At this time they wish to defeat the same-sex parent and gain exclusive access to the opposite-sex parent. When a close attachment is encouraged by the opposite-sex parent and is coupled with a cool, distant relationship with the same-sex parent, a child may develop the sexual identity of the opposite-sex parent. Needless to say, this theory has not been tested or proved and remains inconclusive, yet intriguing.

The most complete attempt to identify contributions to homosexual orientation is reported in *Sexual Preference: Its Development in Men and Women* (Bell, Weinberg and Hammersmith 1981). Based on interviews with 979 homosexual and 477 heterosexual men and women, the authors report that their data do not support traditional psychoanalytic explanations. And social psychological explanations of homosexuality—a lack of adequate heterosexual experiences during childhood, negative experiences with members of the opposite sex, early experiences and contact with homosexuals—are not supported by the evidence either. (For example, many heterosexual adolescents report an occasional sexual interaction with same-sex friends.)

The one social psychological factor that was found to be *somewhat* important was that homosexual men, more than heterosexual men, reported that their fathers were cold and detached. The most consistent finding was that a quarter of the homosexual males showed tendencies *not* to engage in traditionally masculine types of behavior as children. These homosexual men reported a childhood preference for girls' activities, coupled with the feeling that they were not very masculine. Lesbians reported having engaged in homosexual activity during adolescence, and they also expressed gender nonconformity, or dissatisfaction with their own womanhood, more than the heterosexual women in the sample.

In a review of the literature, George Rekers (1986:18) comes to this conclusion: "In light of the contradictory conclusions and lack of good evidence, we believe that it is premature to dogmatically state any explanation of homosexuality which rules out a variety of factors. What actually causes sexual preferences is open to question. Our present understanding of human behavior would suggest that very little of that which we call human behavior is the exclusive product of either biology or culture, but in reality is a result of the interaction between the two."

Christians need to acknowledge the current lack of clear evidence explaining how homosexual orientation develops. We need to develop an approach to homosexuality that is based on a theological and biblical perspective. There are different assessments of the issue within the church. While many Christians believe that homosexual *orientation* is not to be condemned, they do condemn homosexual *behavior* as sin. Other Christians are tolerant of monogamous homosexual expression between consenting adults, but contend it is not what God initially intended for people. Still others accept homosexual expression on par with heterosexual expression and advocate marriage for homosexual couples.

My conviction is that Genesis presents an ideal prototype of complementarity: the male and female become "one flesh" for love, intimacy, union and procreation. And I accept the standard presented in Scripture as normative—God desires sexual intercourse to take place in a mutually exclusive, unconditionally committed heterosexual relationship.

At the same time, I believe it is important to remember that the whole human race is fallen, so none of us achieves absolute sexual wholeness. Homosexual or heterosexual, we all struggle for sexual authenticity. I believe that God is involved in this ongoing process and desires to lead all of us eventually to places of sexual wholeness. This will be a more painful and difficult process for some than for others.

Men in heterosexual relationships. It would be a gross mistake to think that while men in homosexual relationships dishonor God, men in heterosexual relationships always honor God. For as I pointed out earlier in this chapter, men are susceptible to internalizing a variety of sexually distorted views of the male-female relationship. Here, then, I list principles for authenticity in heterosexual relationships.

First, men need to realize that although their natural desire may be to "lord it over" women, this is not God's design for male-female relationships. A husband's attempts to control his wife will sap spontaneity and vitality from their sexual relationship.

Second, men must test their motives for desiring sexual involvement. An inauthentic aspect of male sexuality is the need to gain ego fulfillment by demonstrating sexual prowess. It does something for the male ego to know that he has the power to sexually excite a woman. A man especially feels a sense of power and control when he has brought a woman to such sexual arousal that she can no longer resist his advances.

This kind of ego gratification can be the motive behind sexual involvement. When this happens, sex is separated from personhood, for the goal is not a deeper relationship with the other, but satisfying ego needs.

Third, men must share with women the responsibility for establishing guidelines and setting sexual limits. Christian men must reject the expectation that males should go as far as they can sexually and let females take care of setting boundaries.

For single men, this means that early in a relationship they will openly discuss the values that will guide the sexual aspects of the relationship. Authentic male sexuality leaves no room for trying to intimidate a woman by judging her standards as prudish. It takes an understanding man to want to find out what a particular limit means to his partner. And he needs to be willing to honestly express his own ideas about these standards.

In the end, the man's willingness to honor chosen limits shows the woman that she is valued and cherished. This will deepen the couple's emotional intimacy. It's important that the partners not judge each other for having "stricter" or "looser" standards. The important thing is that each partner be willing to listen to, understand and be open with the other. This is an opportunity to recognize and accept each other's differences—and that is key in all sorts of relationships.

Fourth, a man needs to participate actively in developing *emotional* intimacy with his partner. As discussed in chapter five, men have greater difficulty than women in verbally communicating their feelings. A chief complaint of wives is that their husbands want sex but pay little attention to their emotional needs.

We men must realize that though we feel intimacy while having sex, this may not meet women's intimacy needs. Men who limit their intimacy to sexual encounters are leaving the other dimensions of their relationship undernourished, weak and vulnerable. A full, rich relationship grows as both partners share and get to know each other in all aspects of their lives. Getting to know another person intimately requires listening to the person and learning to appreciate all dimensions of her being. The relationship itself is strengthened in the process of intimate sharing.

Fifth, the foundation of a sexual relationship is mutuality, as expressed in 1 Corinthians 7:4-5: "For the wife does not have authority over her own body, but the husband does; likewise the husband does not have authority over his own body, but the wife does. Do not deprive one another except perhaps by agreement for a set time, to devote yourselves to prayer, and then come together again, so that Satan may not tempt you because of your lack of self-control."

Here we can see that the biblical view of marital sexuality is full mutuality. The words "by agreement" are translated from the Greek word *symphonia*—the same root from which the word "symphony" is derived—which means "with one voice." The mutuality called for in this verse is consonant with Ephesians 5:21, where husbands and wives are told to "be subject to one another out of reverence for Christ."

Authentic marital sexuality occurs when the husband and wife are as "one voice" in their sexual interaction. There is no room for the misguided view that the husband initiates and dominates while the wife submits in obedience. Rather, marital sexuality is to be characterized by mutual desire for lovemaking that is founded on sensitive communication. Just as the orchestra plays as one voice when each instrument contributes its own part and the music is brought together in harmony, so the marital couple reaches sexual harmony through mutuality of sexual expression, communication and sensitive understanding of each other's needs.

Sixth, there will be no game-playing in sexual encounters. There is game-playing when a man intentionally hides his sexual feelings and desires to seek his own advantage. Much game-playing is motivated by inadequate self-esteem. Thus, a partner who does not feel attractive may continually bait the other into affirming him in this area. Another kind of game-playing occurs when partners alternatively show signs of sexual interest and disinterest in each other. This is often motivated by the need to be pursued or the desire to be in control. Game-playing can also take the form of sexual teasing. One partner teases about desiring sex and then resists or is very passive when the other partner makes sexual advances. These games do not enhance the relationship; they end up hurting it.

The seventh principle is that the greater the sensory pleasuring in a relationship outside of coitus, the greater the sexual adequacy. I'm talking about the pleasure of foreplay—the stimulation of erogenous zones of the body before actual intercourse. The lyrics of a popular country-western song express this principle in the vernacular: "I want a man with a slow hand, I want a lover with an easy touch."

Authentic sexuality is much more than intercourse; it involves touch to communicate tenderness, affection, solace, understanding, desire, warmth, comfort and excitement. When partners take time to communicate and learn how to invite and increase responsiveness through touch, they will find more mutual satisfaction.

Eighth, the more secure partners feel in their commitment to each other, the more complete the sexual response will be. Research shows that women especially are most able to invest themselves in a sexual relationship when they feel secure about the relationship. Inversely, a woman who does not trust her spouse or fears that she will lose him is less able to make an adequate sexual response. When security is lacking, there is a tendency toward game-playing.

Shere Hite (1976) found that men, too, desired security in their sexual relationships. Men said they wanted a sexual involvement which made them feel warm and secure, and one that confirmed their masculinity. Here again, we see the critical themes of security and trust to bring about sexual responsiveness and authenticity.

Fighting the Distortions

It's not easy to achieve sexual wholeness when sex is distorted in so many different ways by our culture. As participants in that culture, we'll find some of the distortions creeping into us. We will not always be or behave as the sexually whole person God intends for us to be.

In the past, the Christian community has magnified the "sins of the flesh" out of proportion to other wrongs, giving the wrong impression that sexual sins are far worse than any other sins. It's important to remember that we have been created in the image of God, and we are children of God who have been made righteous through the blood of Christ. *All* our sins are forgivable. Regardless of what our past sexual life has been, we can come before God, ask forgiveness and claim sexual purity in Christ.

At the same time, we are responsible for our sexual behavior. We must earnestly seek God's help to become whole, authentic sexual persons in every aspect of our lives. Although at times we may be tempted to ask God to take away our sexuality, we should instead thank God for this part of our manhood as we seek sexual wholeness.

9
MALE SPIRITUALITY
Renewing the Spirit

The genius of Christianity is that it interconnects the heart, the will, and the divine spirit, and links virtue to surrender. The lesson of Gethsemane is that a man is most virile not when he insists upon his autonomous will but when he harmonizes his will with the will of God.

SAM KEEN, *FIRE IN THE BELLY*

pirituality is the interior life of the soul that governs one's relationship to God. Christian spirituality is the patterning of life around experiences of God in the faith community centered in Christ (Nelson 1988:11-28).

Does God have two different standards of spirituality, one for males and one for females? I would answer with a resounding "No!" The apostle Paul writes, "There is no longer male and female; for all of you are one in Christ Jesus" (Gal 3:28).

Why then a chapter on male spirituality? While it is true that God is "no respecter of persons," it is also true that God allows spirituality to be expressed through the created distinctiveness of maleness and femaleness. Spirituality is not separate from human personhood, but an integral part of it.

The Fall and Male Spirituality
Part of chapter four was devoted to an examination of the Genesis account of the origin of gender differences. It was suggested that Genesis 1:27 must be understood as expressing God's intention that there be

two ways to be human—as a male and as a female. But we also found that the first two chapters of Genesis tell us little about a male as opposed to a female mode of being. The creation account indicates that both Adam and Eve were given dominion over the creatures of the earth, and that both felt no sense of shame as they lived in the Garden. Their life in the Garden before the Fall was good, and they had everything they needed.

The third chapter of Genesis describes Eve and Adam's Fall and its consequences. In these events, I argued in chapter four, we can see the emergence of distinctively male and distinctively female modes of being. At the serpent's suggestion, Eve took the forbidden fruit and ate it; then she gave the fruit to Adam, and he ate it as well. Both Eve and Adam ate the forbidden fruit; they shared equally in the sinful act.

The initial consequences, and their responses, were identical: "Then the eyes of both were opened, and they knew that they were naked; and they sewed fig leaves together and made loincloths for themselves" (Gen 3:7). Later in Genesis 3 we read that Eve and Adam shared three additional consequences: they were both expelled from the Garden, they would both experience struggle and pain in reproducing and feeding their offspring, and they would both experience death. In these ways the Fall affected Adam and Eve the same.

But Genesis 3 also shows us how the Fall affected Adam and Eve in different ways and divided them. As a result of the Fall, *Adam would seek to rule over Eve,* thus disrupting their relationship. In his quest to rule, Adam would create a barrier between himself and Eve—a hindrance to the development of closeness and intimacy. Mary Stewart Van Leeuwen (1990:45) states it this way: "As a result of the Fall there will be a propensity in men to let their dominion run wild, to impose it in cavalier and illegitimate ways not only on the earth and on other men, but also upon the person who is bone of his bones and flesh of his flesh—upon the helper corresponding to his very self. Legitimate, accountable dominion all too easily becomes male domination." Because of the Fall, men, in seeking to dominate, will sabotage closeness and intimacy in relationships.

The result of the Fall on Eve was that she would desire closeness and intimacy with her husband, but could expect to be ruled by him. As Van Leeuwen explains, "The peculiarly female sin . . . is *to use the preservation of . . . relationships as an excuse not to exercise accountable dominion in the first place.* . . . the woman's analogue of the man's congenital flaw, in light of Genesis 3:16, is the temptation to avoid taking risks that might upset relationships. It is the temptation to let creational sociability become fallen 'social enmeshment.' "

In her insightful book *In a Different Voice* (1982), Carol Gilligan lends support to the view that the Fall had differential consequence for males and females. She reports that men more than women struggle with issues of isolation and disconnectedness. As I said before, she reports that men feel the most secure when they have risen to the top and put distance between themselves and others, while women feel safe when they are within a network of others of the same social status. In other words, men are found to have a propensity to distance themselves from others, while women have a propensity to connect with others.

These findings fit with Van Leeuwen's view that the consequence of the Fall for women was a strong desire for connectedness, with the potential of becoming socially enmeshed, while the consequence for men was that they would seek to dominate, and in the process create barriers to closeness and intimacy with others.

If what is being suggested here is true, then men and women are not only different in their disposition to sin, but also in that which constitutes spirituality. Before considering how men and women differ in spirituality, however, we need to examine what the social science literature has to say about male and female differences in moral development.

Developing a Moral Sense

Beginning in the early 1960s, the psychologist Lawrence Kohlberg began to report on his attempts to understand human moral development. According to his theory (1963), moral decision-making is based upon a person's developing reasoning ability. Kohlberg was concerned exclusively with the form of moral reasoning, not with the content. He proposed six sequential stages of moral reasoning, beginning with *punishment and obedience* and progressing to *self-interested exchanges, maintenance of good interpersonal relationships, maintenance of law and order, social contract and individual rights,* and culminating with the highest stage, *universal ethical principles.*

Kohlberg believed that these stages of moral development are invariant for all persons, that no one ever skips a stage and that no one ever reverts to an earlier stage. Although he developed his theory on the basis of research conducted exclusively with men, he argued that his theory was equally applicable to males and females.

As other researchers utilized Kohlberg's instruments to assess moral development in females as well as males, they found that on the average males were at a more "advanced" stage than females. Needless to say, this caused some researchers to wonder whether there was an inherent male bias in the way Kohlberg measured moral development.

The accepted view today is that there is a fundamental difference in the ways males and females make moral decisions. Gilligan (1982) helps clarify this difference. She argues that while males operate in a *reciprocity mode* by stressing rights and justice in making moral decisions, females operate in a *response mode,* emphasizing one's responsibility in the context of personal relationships.

Since Kohlberg studied only men, he found morality to be based on an abstract institutional perspective—concern with rights and justice in society. The ideal in this perspective is equality. In her studies of women and men, Gilligan found that women's decisions and actions are embedded in the personal relationships that provide the meaningful context of their lives.

For example, in facing real-life decisions about abortion, men were prone to decide on the basis of abstract principles—whether abortion is morally right or wrong. Women, on the other hand, were more likely to base their decisions on the concrete personal circumstances of the situation. Women tended to ask questions about the effect of an abortion, or lack of it, on the personal relationships of those involved. Men often stuck to asking abstract questions, such as whether the termination of the life of a fetus should be considered murder.

Gender Differences in Spirituality

The differences in the way men and women relate and make moral decisions have implications for spirituality. I believe that female spirituality more than male spirituality is tied in with relational issues. For women, spirituality is experienced in close and harmonious relationships with God and with others. Women will also gauge spirituality on the basis of *being* in relationship, rather than in terms of *doing*. Female spirituality is most likely to include the spiritual disciplines of meditation and devotion, and active fellowship with others, particularly other women (in Bible studies, luncheons, workshops, conferences, retreats, and the like).

For men, spirituality is experienced more in terms of holding to and acting upon right values and beliefs. Men will gauge their spirituality on the basis of spiritual *understanding and knowledge, accomplishments* and *activities*. Male spirituality will more likely include the spiritual disciplines of prayer, Bible study and asceticism. In relationships, men will place a greater emphasis on active *doing*—serving God and others—than on merely being in relationship.

A missionary friend of mine noted that on the mission field there is a common tendency for men to develop programs and other ministry structures (Bible schools, training centers and administrative functions) that placed them in positions of authority and distanced them from nationals. Women missionaries were more commonly involved in personal work in the community and church fellowship.

To more fully understand the difference between male and female spirituality, we need to consider gender-based differences in spiritual strengths and vulnerabilities. The first column of table 2 is a comparative summary of male and female spiritual strengths.

Based on Scripture references such as 2 Corinthians 6:17, "Therefore come out from them, and be separate from them, says the Lord," there is a rich tradition of Christian spirituality that emphasizes separating from the world. Given males' tendency to have developed a healthy dose of differentiation from parents and family, it's not surprising that they would be better prepared psychologically to live a life of separation from others. In the history of both the Eastern Orthodox church and the

---

Table 2. Gender Differences in Spiritual Strengths and Vulnerabilities

	Potential Spiritual Strengths	Potential Spiritual Vulnerabilities
Males	Separation from the world Strong sense of self Desire to be filled with the Holy Spirit and act with power Bible study: Quest for right answers	Pride in self Tendency to magnify own power Quest for power, prestige, righteousness Tendency to manipulate others Fortress mentality
Females	Spirituality defined by being Openness to spiritual interdependence Openness to being used by the Spirit Bible study: Quest for right relationships	Lack of differentiation and individuation Tendency to enmeshment, triviality and diffuseness Dependence on others for self- definition Gossipy sociability Inability to respect standards of privacy

---

Roman Catholic church, monasticism has been the main path men have chosen to obtain spirituality.

It's true that within the Roman Catholic church women have also separated themselves from worldly cares by becoming nuns. Significantly, however, the vows women take in becoming nuns make a greater emphasis upon entering into a spiritual union with God. Nuns aspire to become the bride of Christ. For women, then, spiritual maturity is more likely to be conceptualized as being in a right relationship with God.

Monks generally devoted themselves to accomplishing *tasks*—copying the entire Bible in longhand or praying for a number of hours each day. Monks were also more likely to seek spirituality through an isolated solitary life, as exemplified by the Eastern Orthodox monks who to this day live alone on mountain pinnacles on the coast of Greece.

Differences between men and women can also be seen in the degree to which they nurture their spiritual life in association with others. When men enter into small-group Bible studies, they are often seeking answers to questions about their Christian faith. Women are more likely to value sharing groups and Bible studies for the relationships they develop within them. Women find it easier than men to share spiritual concerns and to enter into prayer with others.

In informal surveys, I've found that many Christian women desire times when they can pray with their husbands, but most Christian husbands find it hard to pray with their wives. If you do not think this is true, I challenge you to ask Christian couples who has the greater desire to pray together, husbands or wives. When two people come before God together, they enter into a form of spiritual intimacy. And men more than women have difficulty with intimacy, including spiritual intimacy.

In Eastern religions, salvation comes to the person who realizes that the autonomous self is an illusion and one is merely a part of god or the eternal force of the universe. Christian salvation, on the other hand, is relational; it comes when one chooses to allow oneself to become rightly related to God. The implications of this for discovering true manhood are expressed by Gordon Dalbey (1988:28) as follows: "What if, indeed, authentic manhood can be approached only in relationship with the Father God, who seeks in every man to fulfill the purpose for which He has created him? If so, true manhood is not something to be sought, but to be revealed, precisely as a man submits to the God who called him into being and in whom lies his ultimate destiny."

Because men generally develop a greater degree of individuation, they tend to have a stronger sense of self. This stronger sense of self gives them a firm basis on which to build a right relationship with God. Men may thus be better able to avoid enmeshment in relating to God and others. Women may have more of a tendency toward enmeshment in spiritual relationships, as they do in the social dimensions of their relationships.

Spiritual mentoring, or spiritual direction, is an important way we can open our lives to one another and grow closer to God. Women may be better able to begin a mentoring relationship than men, but perhaps they are more vulnerable to dependency tendencies within it. Although men may be less vulnerable to enmeshment, they may miss what mentoring can give them because they fail to even enter into it.

Another spiritual strength of men can be seen in their desire to be filled with the Holy Spirit and act with power. Christian men desire to be potent and effective. As I once heard an evangelist proclaim, "God wants you to be *gorged* by the Holy Spirit and do great and mighty things for the Lord!"

Men tend to concentrate on what they can accomplish for God. Churchmen through history have been preoccupied with building bigger and better churches, higher and higher steeples. Current mission leaders note a drive for heroics in the new generation of young missionaries—they want to be a part of a movement that is doing great things for God. Men are also the driving force behind the contemporary church-growth movement.

Men are attracted to a church where they can join in accomplishing things. Women are more attracted to a church because of the warmth and security of relationships they can find there. In general, women tend to value right relationships over right theology.

Presented in column two of table 2 is a comparative summary of male and female spiritual vulnerabilities. Male spiritual vulnerabilities are the shadow side of male spiritual strengths. The very masculine quality that constitutes a spiritual strength can become a vulnerability when it is fueled by the wrong motive. This is something of what Paul had in mind when he wrote, "Knowledge puffs up, but love builds up" (1 Cor 8:1). Paul certainly was not saying that knowledge in and of itself is bad; in fact, he urges believers to *know* the Scriptures. Knowledge is good, but when we possess knowledge we may be vulnerable to vanity and pride.

In the same way, the male strength of individuation can lead to a pride in self, a tendency to trust in self-sufficiency rather than in God. Dalbey (1988:28) suggests that self-sufficiency is especially a cultural trap for men in Western societies:

Unlike Third World men, who recognize and respond out of spiritual reality, we "modern-scientific" men have fearfully avoided facing spiritual power, because it shatters our treasured goal-image of rational self-sufficiency. In our God-created hearts, we know that genuine manhood is rooted in mysteries which no logic or computer program can comprise. The spiritual dimension to manhood thereby reminds us of our inadequacy, and we prefer to ignore if not suppress it altogether.

From self-sufficiency it is but a small step to developing a fortress mentality. Men have not only devoted great efforts to building military fortresses to protect themselves from physical attack but have built up a fortress mentality to protect themselves from spiritual attack. Separating from the world in order to give the whole of one's life and thoughts to God can be the highest of spiritual goals. But separation can also be motivated by the desire to rid oneself of all temptations.

Men more than women tend to externalize temptation, ascribing it to external objects. Having externalized temptation, men believe that the way to live a pure and holy life is to build a fortress around oneself—hiding behind thick monastery walls, in the seclusion of the wilderness or on an inaccessible mountaintop. Men whose spirituality is dependent upon a fortress mentality are likely to develop a false sense of security. A fortress mentality can also be a defense against the risks and discomforts of opening oneself to other men and being known by them. As Dalbey (1988:31) says,

> If truth is the power which God invests primarily in masculinity, then we fear being with other men because together the uncomfortable truths about us shall be revealed. Only as we surrender our self-centered pride to God, therefore, can we begin to base our confidence among other men not upon our own ability to destroy, but upon God's ability to create. Instead of defending ourselves from the truth, we can appropriate the courage and strength we share, and work together to improve our common welfare.

Feeling protected from the "things of the world" can leave one open for Satan's temptation to yield to the sin of pride. Having externalized and objectified their sins, men are vulnerable to the more subtle sins of feeling invincible, self-sufficient, powerful and above reproach.

Men's desire to do great and mighty things for the Lord clearly has a flip side of spiritual vulnerability. The quest for bigger churches and larger congregations can be motivated by a minister's psychological need for power, prestige and accomplishment. Men whose identity is in Jesus Christ can accept themselves for who they are and are free to do great and mighty things for *God's* glory. But men who are still struggling to accept their own identity must accomplish great things as proof *to themselves* that they are worthy of God's acceptance.

More than a few years ago, Bishop Fulton Sheen wryly said that men who were obsessed with building expensive, lavish church buildings had "edifice complexes." Men more than women seem to be vulnerable to the need to accomplish in order to prove themselves to themselves.

The Spiritual Warrior

While the role of the warrior was denigrated within the early men's movement, it is included as a respectable aspect of the male psyche by the new men's movement. Within Scripture, spiritual warfare is understood as part of spirituality, and Christians are called to be spiritual warriors.

I believe it's helpful for men to accept the identity of a spiritual warrior as long as they resist the secular view of what a warrior is. Men in the early men's movement were right in rejecting the secular culture's "macho" warrior image, epitomized by Rambo. Compare this violent machine-gun warrior to the spiritual warrior described in Ephesians 6:10-18:

Finally, be strong in the Lord and in the strength of his power. Put on the whole armor of God, so that you may be able to stand against the wiles of the devil. For our struggle is not against enemies of blood and flesh, but against the rulers, against the authorities, against the cosmic powers of this present darkness, against the spiritual forces of evil in the heavenly places. Therefore take up the whole armor of God, so that you may be able to withstand on that evil day, and having done everything, to stand firm. Stand therefore, and fasten the belt of truth around your waist, and put on the breastplate of righteousness. As shoes for your feet put on whatever will make you ready to proclaim the gospel of peace. With all of these, take the shield of faith, with which you will be able to quench all the flaming arrows of the evil one. Take the helmet of salvation, and the sword of the Spirit, which is the word of God.

Pray in the Spirit at all times in every prayer and supplication. To that end keep alert and always persevere in supplication for all the saints.

Although the warrior of Ephesians is strong, note that his strength is derived from God's mighty power. This warrior is armed for both defensive and offensive battle, but note what the armor consists of—truth, righteousness, the gospel of peace, faith, salvation, the Holy Spirit and prayer.

Taking up the true armor of God, we must reject any sort of coercive, violent, oppressive or domineering view of spiritual warfare. The history of the Christian church is unfortunately full of men who carried out grand inquisitions, organized witch hunts, burned "heretics" at the stake and enacted other cruel forms of violence, all in the name of spiritual warfare.

After graduating from high school, a schoolmate and I attended a Bible college for two years. Returning home for the summer, armed with one whole year of Bible-school training, we were called upon to give sermons in small rural churches. Each of us perfected one sermon that we gave repeatedly. To this day I still remember my buddy Morris's sermon—"Flee, Follow and Fight." His text was 1 Timothy 6:11-12, where Paul is writing to Timothy on the topic of spirituality.

Paul had it right! We are engaged in a spiritual battle. But, as I can still hear Morris preach the text, the key to being a spiritual warrior is knowing when to *flee,* when to *follow* and when to *fight.* Paul advises Timothy to flee from the quest for fulfillment through riches and personal gain. Instead, we are to follow after righteousness, godliness, faith, love, endurance and gentleness. The spiritual warrior needs to incorporate these qualities into his character. Only then is he ready to fight the good fight of faith.

We men need to understand the balance between fleeing, following and fighting. The soft male may want to flee, the macho male may be eager to fight. The man of God needs to do both while *following* Christ's example.

Male Spirituality in Action

I have learned a lot about male spirituality by watching men at conferences and retreats. About a year ago I was asked to speak at a men's retreat sponsored by the Southern California region of a Protestant denomination. I picked up a hint that this might be a little out of the ordinary when, two months before the retreat, the pastor in charge called to tell me that a group of men in his church had committed themselves to pray for me *daily*. I was told that they were praying that God would do a mighty work through me in the lives of the men who would be at the retreat.

Wow! Talk about pressure! I began to wonder, "What if God doesn't do any obvious mighty work through me? Will these men then assume that I was the barrier to God's working in their midst?" I found myself beginning to pray that God *would* use me as an instrument of his hands at the retreat. As I look back, I must say that my prayers were probably motivated more from my fear of failing to live up to their expectations than out of a real concern for the men themselves.

A week before the conference, I got a phone call telling me that the men had been encouraged to invite non-Christian friends to the conference—and that a number of non-Christian men would indeed be coming. Again, I was assured of their expectation that God would do marvelous things at the conference. Needless to say, my anxiety level went up about one hundred per cent.

But why worry when you can pray? My anxiety served as an effective, if questionable, motivation for praying even more fervently. A few days before the conference I leveled with the Lord: "Oh God, you can't let me down! You've got to do something at the conference that will be perceived by these men as a mighty work." As I tried to get beyond my self-centered concerns, God allowed me to genuinely pray for openness in the hearts and minds of the men at the conference.

On the Friday afternoon of the conference, I began the two-hour trip into the San Bernardino Mountains on my faithful 1976 750cc Honda motorcycle. As the traffic on the freeway was already getting heavy at two in the afternoon, I was glad I had left early. I intended to arrive at the conference grounds in plenty of time to prepare myself emotionally and spiritually before the first meeting in the evening.

About thirty miles out of Pasadena, with the mountains beginning to loom through the smog in the distance, my motorcycle stopped. After five frustrating minutes of trying to kick-start it, I drew upon my limited automotive knowledge to diagnose a dead battery. Following a two-mile walk to the nearest freeway exit, I used a public telephone to contact what I *thought* was the nearest motorcycle shop.

To make a long story short, I arrived at the conference just minutes before the start of the first meeting. With grease and dirt on my hands and arms, and sweat rolling down my face, I grumbled, "Lord, this is a fine way to start a conference."

The first session went well; the men seemed to empathize as I explained why I had arrived in such disarray. After a good night's sleep, I felt much better and appreciated the men's warmth and receptiveness at the morning meetings.

The afternoon was spent in good-natured sports competition. At the Saturday-evening meeting I sensed a real openness as I challenged the men to examine their own definition of manhood and how it affected their relationships. Following my presentation, the pastor in charge invited those who would like to receive Jesus Christ as their personal Savior to come forward. I thought, "Oh no, what is he going to think of my effectiveness if no one comes forward?" As it turned out, five men prayed for a new life in Christ.

After the meeting, we loaded up with hot chocolate and doughnuts and hiked to an outdoor circle where a huge fire was blazing. Accompanied by several guitars, we sang gospel songs in the crisp night air under a cloudless starry sky.

After a few songs, one of the one hundred men around the campfire said that he wanted to share something. He began haltingly, appearing to assess how much he could trust the rest of us. His story unfolded with much pain, as he told how he'd recently learned that his seventeen-year-old son was addicted to crack and how his wife was threatening to leave him. Seeking relief from his pain, he had turned to alcohol. He broke down and let out a great cry of pain.

Quickly, six or seven men put their arms around this hurting brother. Keeping him in a warm embrace, first one began to pray for him, and then another, and another, and another.

After a season of prayer, another man shared his decision to accept Christ that night. He said he had come to the retreat at the invitation of his neighbor George. He told of watching George suffer the loss of his nine-year-old son to cancer the previous year. What impressed him most was how George had continued in his faith *after* his son had been taken from him. This, he said, caused him to be open to George's invitation and faith.

At this point, George emerged from the darkness around the fire and, with tears rolling down his cheeks, gave his new brother in Christ a big hug. Other men followed George's example, using bear hugs to welcome their new brother into Christ's kingdom.

We stayed around the bonfire for another hour and a half, as the cycle of sharing, praying and hugging was repeated again and again.

As I walked back to my cabin in the cold night air, I thought, "This is male spirituality in action." These men had not only been bold enough to pray in faith for great and mighty things, but they had been willing to go beyond the safe boundaries of traditional male spirituality by sharing their personal pain and concern for one another. Those who expressed their pain were not only prayed for but also physically comforted by other men. I think males hunger for this kind of intimacy, but most of us rarely get it.

It's good to recognize that men may have distinctive spiritual strengths and vulnerabilities, but we shouldn't fatalistically accept any masculine stereotype. Rather, because we know that men have difficulty in becoming intimately connected in relationships, we need to intentionally create situations that will facilitate connection.

Men need to pray for other men and hear other men's prayers. Men need to hug other men and in turn experience warm, strong physical support from them. Wives need to hear their husbands' expressions of love, and husbands need to hear love from their wives. Fathers need warm hugs from their children, and their children need to feel the tender strength of their fathers' bodies.

As we seek spiritual growth, we can look to our model of full male spirituality: the man who, according to Mark (10:16), took children "in his arms, laid his hands on them, and blessed them."

10
STAGES OF A MAN'S LIFE
Growing Through Crisis

For everything there is a season, and a time for every matter under heaven: a time to be born, and a time to die.

ECCLESIASTES 3:1-2

The first forty years of life give us the text; the next thirty supply the commentary.

ARTHUR SCHOPENHAUER

B
eing born a male does not make one a *man*. Nor does merely getting older automatically make a male mature.

Being a man is a socially defined category denoting a status of maturity. To the Plains Indian boy, being a man is to be old enough to go along on the hunt. To the Samoan Island boy, being a man is to be old enough to go out on the fishing boats. And so it goes in most societies: being a man is associated with being allowed to play some useful role alongside other men. Since physical maturity seems to set the pace of social and emotional development, most men reach manhood along with others of the same age.

In nonindustrial societies, the male life cycle consists of two major stages—boyhood and manhood. In industrialized societies, however, there are more discretely identifiable life-cycle stages. As we have come to understand the important cultural, social and psychological forces associated with these stages, it's become clear that the transition from one life-cycle stage to the next is not always smooth. In fact, transitions between stages are often called "periods of crisis."

My goal in this chapter is to explain the major life-cycle stages and to sensitize males as to how they can experience movement from one stage to another as growth rather than crisis.

Stages of a Man's Life

My father used to say, "I don't get older, I get better." There is much truth in such a statement, for life experience brings the possibility for an integrated maturity that can be gained in no other way. The puzzle is why some men experience getting older as getting better while for others it means getting worse.

The seminal writings of Erik Erikson (1963) began to unlock this puzzle. Erikson conceptualized human development as progressing through sequential stages of development. For some, each new stage of life and its changes are growth-producing experiences, while for others such changes become obstacles that lead to deterioration. Building upon Erikson's work, Daniel Levinson (1978) studied the lives of adult men and found key transition periods that men must move through to get from one stage to the next.

Based upon the perspectives of these two men, other scholars have worked hard to challenge, support, revise and refine the concept of human developmental stages. I believe the concept of stage development can help us understand regular patterns of development in our lives—as long as we don't try to apply the concepts too rigidly.

Men enter and exit from the developmental stages at different ages. Some men move from one stage to another so quickly that it doesn't even make sense to speak of two separate life-cycle stages. Some men linger in a given stage, and some seem to "get stuck," unable to move on. Some men will experience a major crisis during an early transition, but find later transitions relatively easy. Other men seem to be able to avoid any transitional crisis until their move to retirement.

So take note: the material I present in this chapter identifies the major issues and patterns that most men will experience, but it does not line out changes that all men will pass through in lock-step unison.

Table 3 provides an overview of the developmental changes in a man's life. The major developmental stages are given in column one;

column two gives the approximate age span for each stage. Presented in column three are the major developmental tasks that Erikson associates with each stage. Finally, column four lists the major transitional stages, as suggested by Levinson, that males experience in their journey through life.

Table 3. Developmental Changes in a Man's Life

Developmental Stage	Approximate Age	Major Developmental Tasks (Erikson)	Major Transitions (Levinson)
Childhood	0-12	Trust, Autonomy, Initiative and Industry	
Adolescence	13-19	Identity	Early Adult
Young Adulthood	20-29	Intimacy	Age 30
Middle Adulthood	30-45	Generativity	Midlife
Mature Adulthood	46-65	Ego Integration	Age 50
Late Adulthood	66+	Late Adult	

Childhood: Boys Will Be Boys

From the day children are born, society puts its expectations and its imprint upon them. Little boys are expected to behave like boys, and little girls like girls. That this is so was demonstrated by a simple but creative study in which the names on the cribs of infants in a hospital viewing room were switched. All the boy babies were assigned female names, and the girl babies were assigned male names. The researchers then sat back to record the comments made by friends and relatives who came to view the infants. Viewers described the boy babies as "cute," "darling," "so sweet and gentle," "looks just like her mother," while the girls were called "robust, "a real tiger," "strong" and "energetic."

What begins as an expectation soon becomes a self-fulfilling prophecy—the expectation succeeds in bringing about the expected behavior. Sure enough, boys will be boys.

As boys emerge from infancy into early childhood, they begin to internalize an image of masculine behavior that includes anger, boisterous humor, competitive or athletic enthusiasm, physical or verbal aggression and similar "manly" traits. They come to reject "feminine" traits—tenderness, compassion, sentimentality, gentleness, verbal affection, soft-heartedness and the like—believing that these are to be avoided at all costs.

As the boy moves out from under the family umbrella and into the sphere of male peer groups, the taboo against expressing any feeling characteristic of girls is reinforced and continued. To be affectionate, gentle and expressive toward others is not being "one of the boys." The mass media seem to convey a similar message. From comics and cartoons through more "adult" fare, the male image does not usually include affectionate, tender or soft-hearted behavior—unless it happens to come from a very small boy (for adults to appreciate, not as a model for other young boys) or from a gray-haired grandfather.

Family, peer group and mass media, then, converge to play the tune to which the male must dance. Confronted with the image projected by this powerful triumvirate, most young males quickly learn that whatever masculine behavior *is*, it *is not* an expression of gentleness, tenderness, compassion, verbal affection or love.

Erikson divides childhood into four developmental stages, beginning with children's need during the first year of life to develop basic *trust.* If a child's caretakers provide a safe, stable, secure environment, the child develops a sense of inner security. The world is experienced as a friendly place where people can be relied upon.

Trust is the necessary basis for the development of secure bonding between children, irrespective of gender, and their caretakers. Children who are deprived of trusting and caring relationships may be hindered from developing a mature faith and trusting relationship with God. The ability to experience God as a loving and trustworthy Father is related to having had a loving, trusting relationship with human parents or caretakers. The child who is deprived of trust during this first year of life carries this deficiency into the next developmental stage.

When basic trust has been established during the first year of life, children have the foundational security needed to enter the next stage of development—*autonomy.* Sometime during the second year of life, children abandon their clinging dependence in favor of a fierce independence, wanting to do things their own way. During the stage of autonomy children will reject parents' offers of help, asserting, "No, I do myself!" "I tie shoes!" or simply "No!"

Is it any wonder that this stage has been informally labeled "the terrible twos"? Most two-year-old children want to do everything themselves their own way. Wise parents will be able to give guidance and control while letting the child develop needed freedom and autonomy. As discussed in chapter two, boys may have a built-in tendency toward separateness, while girls may have a pull toward continued connectedness. Whether these are genuine natural tendencies or not, parents tend to be more tolerant of boys' autonomy demands than girls'. This leads to a greater spirit of adventure among males—a difference between males and females that seems to remain throughout life.

The child who has mastered autonomy is set to tackle the third of Erikson's developmental stages—*initiative*. Children ages three to five are full of wonder and discovery. They possess a natural curiosity that moves them into an ever-expanding social world. Their main question is *WHY?* They want to know why things are done as they are, and why they can or can't do certain things.

In a healthy social environment, children are challenged to be active and to master new skills. In an atmosphere of approval and acceptance, children will take the initiative to dress themselves, put their own clothes and toys away and generally assume responsibility for their own lives. Parents can discourage initiative in their children in a number of ways—remaking a child's bed because it is not done right, failing to affirm a child's effort to pick up his own toys, or criticizing the way a child completes a task.

During the initiative stage, many parents encourage gender-stereotyped activity in their children. Girls are encouraged to concentrate on domestic-oriented tasks—cooking, making a bed, sweeping a room or caring for a younger brother or sister. Parents affirm boys for accomplishing such tasks as riding a bike, fixing a toy or carrying firewood into the house. The bottom line is that boys emerge from this third developmental stage with greater initiative in tasks that have been defined for them as "masculine," while girls have been encouraged to take greater initiative in "feminine" areas.

Beginning around age six, children enter the fourth developmental stage, which Erikson called *industry*. As they begin school and explore the wider world, children become preoccupied with the manner in which things are made and operate. If children are encouraged during this stage, they will take pride in their ability to learn. Children who don't receive encouragement from parents or teachers will lack a well-developed sense of industry.

Research shows that boys develop greater industry toward the external world of objects and things and experience achievement by developing physical skills and athletic prowess. Girls, on the other hand, begin to develop skills in interpersonal relationships and classroom achievement. Beginning in the first grade, girls earn higher grades than boys, a pattern that persists until college.

Adolescence: No Longer a Boy, Not Yet a Man

When children begin their teenage years, they move from industry to the developmental stage of *identity*. This is an important stage to understand for masculine development because of the differing ways identity is formed in males and females. Adolescence is an especially problematic time for males because of the nature of modern industrial society.

Social origins of adolescence. Before the Industrial Revolution, there were no adolescents, only children and adults. Rites of passage were well defined, for once boys had undergone puberty rites they were welcomed into society as *men*. Even today, this is largely true in nonindustrial societies.

Industrialization and urbanization have brought a slower and more ambiguous passage into adulthood. With the development of factories, the apprenticeship system—whereby boys learned their trade under the watchful eye of a master craftsman—declined. During the early stage of industrialization, youth began to leave their homes to take unskilled factory jobs in cities. They worked long hours for very low pay, lived together in urban slum apartments and gradually became alienated from the rest of society. With this disfranchisement from adult life, they became a problem that was labeled "adolescence."

This period of development, which initially encompassed just a few urban boys for a brief period of their lives, has grown to include virtually all youth in our society. The gap between childhood and adulthood that we call adolescence is also expanding. One reason for this is the decline in unskilled jobs, with a concomitant increase in jobs that require skill and education. To gain meaningful employment today, males must continue their education and delay their entrance into the full-time work force, from which they derive adult status. And except in farm families, most work is now done outside the home. This means that fathers are unable to provide a visible work model for their sons.

Other important factors are the replacement of the extended family by the nuclear family and the increasing numbers of one-parent families. In nine out of ten cases one-parent families mean father-absent families. Adolescent boys especially suffer from the lack of a live-in father to model manhood for them.

Each of these factors contributes to the confusion adolescent boys feel in growing up. Where there is no clearly written script, growing up is an absurd experience—like being handed an instrument and being told to play without a musical score to follow. Given that there are no clear cultural norms, much rapid change in fashions and style, as well as "getting into trouble" behavior, can be understood as adolescent boys' searching for and improvising new types of behavior.

Not only is our society unclear in defining what it expects from adolescents, but it's also contradictory. In terms of voting privileges and military service, an eighteen-year-old is judged to be an adult. In most states a boy can't get a driving permit until sixteen. But the age of adulthood *drops* when it becomes financially profitable. Movie theaters, airlines and most public establishments that require an admission fee consider a twelve-year-old to be an adult. Teenagers are asked to pay adult prices, but when it comes to adult privileges, they are told to wait until they grow up.

Identity crisis. As a result of the social structural origins of adolescence described above, adolescence is experienced as an identity crisis. Indeed, Erikson believed that identity is the primary developmental task teenagers are working through. In Erikson's scheme, both males and females needed to work through identity as adolescents, followed by intimacy during their early adult years. According to some research, this is true of males, but adolescent females are likely to be working through intimacy issues either before or along with identity issues.

While adolescent girls are typically involved in a changing network of four to six "best" female friends, males form groups that endure over longer periods of time. Up until their teenage years, boys gain their sense of identity primarily in relationship to their family. At the onset of adolescence they begin a "desatellization" process, away from the pull of their family. Now they begin to orbit around their peer group.

Adolescent boys develop a sense of identity and self-worth based on their status *within* their peer group. Here they can compete for status on a more equal footing than they could in their families, where their parents and older siblings have an advantage. Achieving status within the peer group also begins a competitive process whereby males establish themselves in a "pecking" order. Adolescent males are so preoccupied with finding their identity that they have very little energy left to develop intimacy skills.

The key developmental task for adolescent boys is to consolidate all knowledge they have gained about themselves. This involves integrating the various self-images they have accumulated into a personal identity with awareness of a past and a future.

When the boy cannot manage to pull all his identities together into one integrated whole, a crisis of "identity diffusion" can result. An adolescent boy's sense of personal identity needs to include appropriate identification of an adult gender role. If an adequate masculine identity is taking root, then the personality develops a healthy, harmonious blend of sexually defined qualities. Failure to achieve a clear, appropriate sexual identity can adversely affect a male's overall ego identity.

Although successful adolescence originates in early childhood, the male's sense of personal identity is significantly affected by his status in his peer group. Adolescent females are oriented more toward interpersonal relationships than peer group status. Correspondingly, they are less preoccupied with forming an identity than they are with developing intimacy skills. Not surprisingly, males enter young adulthood with less-developed intimacy skills than females.

Young Adulthood: A Man at Last

The male who emerges from adolescence with a coherent, integrated sense of self is prepared to develop intimacy skills. Two barriers, competition and homophobia, can work against males' achieving intimacy with others (chapter twelve discusses these barriers more fully).

Whereas intimacy between young women is based upon verbal communication and emotional sharing, young men are likely to feel that they are intimate when they are merely with other males, or doing things with them. A young man's intimacy with women can be hindered by the male tendency to sexualize opposite-gender friendships (see chapter thirteen for a fuller discussion of this). Males with undeveloped intimacy skills will especially tend to equate sexual involvement with intimacy.

With better-developed intimacy skills, females in their early twenties are usually more capable of distinguishing between sexual involvement and emotional intimacy than are males of the same age. Differing levels of identity and intimacy development are responsible for many of the struggles young adult males and females experience as they attempt to build relationships with each other.

Based on his interviews with adult males, Levinson identifies two additional developmental tasks facing young men. The first is to move out of the pre-adult world. For some men between the ages of seventeen and twenty-two, this can be a struggle. Related to this is the developmental task of taking preliminary steps to enter the adult world. This involves going to college, gaining a full-time job or getting an apartment of one's own.

Young men may feel ambivalent about leaving adolescence behind and moving out into the adult world. A twenty-one-year-old male, who several years earlier couldn't wait to leave home, compares the comforts of his room at home and Mom's good cooking with the expenses and hassles of living on his own and wonders what the hurry is. I've noticed that more than a few parents have had to remove some of the feathers from the nest to encourage their grown son to leave home.

The accomplishment of the two tasks identified by Levinson constitutes what he calls *early adult transition* (age seventeen to twenty-two). During this transition, youth are formally granted the symbols of adulthood, such as the privileges to vote and buy liquor. But informally, young people of this age may still be treated as adolescents if they have not yet obtained the two most important symbols of adulthood—marriage and a full-time job.

Once the transition has been made to early adulthood, young men between the ages of twenty-two and twenty-eight need to set about developing a workable adult life structure. This can include gaining a full-time job, living on one's own and getting married. There may be a tentativeness during this period as young men explore possibilities. They may want to keep their options open in order to avoid "premature" strong commitments. During this period, men balance the need to create structure with the need to keep their options open. Thus, leaving young adulthood can be experienced as both exciting and confusing.

Middle Adulthood: Running as Fast as I Can

Middle adulthood begins with the *age thirty transition,* which extends from roughly age twenty-eight to age thirty-three. As he moves out of his twenties, a man comes to realize that there is little time left to change his life structure. Rather than trying to "keep options open," he may begin to feel that "this is the last chance." For one dissatisfied with his occupation, there may be the feeling that this is the last chance to do what he really wants to do. This is a time of re-evaluation in which a man may consider new choices, but conclude that he is satisfied with life choices he has made.

Following the age thirty transition comes the *settling-down* period (ages thirty-three to thirty-nine). In this second attempt at adult life structure, a man invests himself deeply in work, family, friendships, leisure, community or whatever is most important to him. The tentativeness of his early structure is gone. On his job a man will strive to prove to himself that he can make it. He may earnestly begin to climb the occupational ladder. In family life, the demands of fathering call him to spend time with his children—to play with them, take them camping overnight, become a Scoutmaster or coach a Little League team. During this period men are very busy and committed to building their life structure. Toward the end of the settling-down period, a man may begin to assess the progress he has made in light of the goals he had set for himself.

Midlife crisis. With the end of the settling-down period comes the age forty to forty-five *midlife transition.* For most men the midlife transition is the "big one"—point 8 or above on the Richter earthquake scale.

A number of factors make it likely that this transition will become a crisis. The most important factor is the rapidity of social and technological change. Personal and occupational crises develop when men are unprepared for changes in their world. Men in the labor force today are especially vulnerable; the job for which they have been trained can become obsolete through the latest technological innovation. Automobile workers, for example, experience understandable anxiety when they realize that robots can do the type of work they were trained to do. A similar anxiety plagues men in white-collar occupations when they see a highly trained specialist using a computer to do the work previously done by ten men. Men at managerial levels have the fear of being "overtaken" by younger, better-trained college graduates—including young women!

Midlife transition can also be a crisis for the man who realizes that he will not reach the lofty goal he had set for himself. To him, reaching this goal had become the criterion he used to judge himself as worthy and valuable. Not reaching the goal creates a crisis of self-esteem.

Other men may feel that they did their best work at an earlier age and that life is now downhill and boring. The term *career burnout* has been coined to refer to such situations. Some compare the progress of their career with the progress of others of a similar age and become discouraged because they have not accomplished as much. These people feel that they are not on schedule with their accomplishments.

Still others, who have devoted long hours to their jobs, reach midlife and realize that they've spent little time with their children. Some find that when they attempt to reach out, their now nearly grown children are unresponsive. Other hardworking fathers find that when they want to relax with their wife and children, they are unable to do so. The crisis in this case is that they have become slaves to work and career. They have become workaholics.

Four polarities that can intensify crisis. In his study of career-oriented men, Levinson (1978:209-44) has identified four polarities of midlife transition. Although these polarities exist through the entire adult life cycle of men, they are accentuated during transition periods. Men who have dealt with these polarities throughout their lives, having met minor crises on a regular basis, do not experience the midlife transition as a crisis period. On the other hand, men who have not dealt with these polarities are candidates for a major midlife crisis.

Men in midlife can feel quite unsettled because of the *young/old* polarity. These men feel older than young men, but they are not ready to join the rocking-chair set just yet. One sign of this concern is that these men will attempt to appear younger than they are. They may dress in a sporty style or put themselves on a rigorous weight-lifting and running routine to help them look young.

The second polarity is *destruction/creation.* Having experienced conflict on the job and being battle-scarred and hurt by others, men in midlife may resort to the same tactics. They are also aware of the heart attacks and even deaths of friends their age. At the same time they have a strong desire to be creative. Having accumulated the needed training and experience, professional men look to midlife and beyond as the time when they will reach their peak in creativity and productivity.

In terms of the *masculinity/femininity* polarity, middle-aged men may want to sustain their manly appearance of strength and toughness, but at the same time they develop a desire to become more nurturing. Their masculine side pushes them to further achievement and ambition, while their feminine side calls them to be more relational and sensitive to the needs of others.

Finally, the *attachment/separateness* polarity points to the need to find a balance between being connected to others and being self-sufficient. A man has a high need for attachment during the early part of his career, because he needs to learn from others who are more experienced. There comes a point when this same man needs to pull away, to be in charge or at least to have the opportunity to try out his own ideas.

During any transition, men need to confront a polarity as they become aware of it. Growth can come when a man finds a new way of being young, masculine, creative or attached. There is nothing wrong with a middle-aged man's wish to stay young, but he must not allow himself to be stuck in a particular way of being young. At the age of fifty-three, I still enjoy playing intramural flag football with the students at Fuller Seminary. When I came to Fuller ten years ago, my body was still (barely) agile enough to play quarterback. Eight years ago I dislocated a knee, but I got a knee brace and continued playing quarterback. After a few years of struggling, I realized that I was stuck in my attempt to be young. Since I gave up my need to be quarterback, I began to enjoy playing other positions—I learned to be young in a new way.

Erikson uses the term *generativity* to refer to the major developmental task that men must master during their middle adulthood years. Generativity is possible to the extent that each of the four polarities is confronted and dealt with creatively. The opposite of generativity is *stagnation,* the state of not growing, being bogged down, static, stuck. Middle-aged men are living out generativity when they invest themselves in other people and delight in seeing their work and ideas live on through them. The principal characteristic of a generative man is that he is a man who lives *for* others.

Middle-aged men have the knowledge and experience to be influential—to have power over others. Men who use power to control others are acting from the basis of stagnation. Men who use power to empower others are processing generativity. (See chapter seven for a full discussion of empowering.)

Mature Adulthood: Sometimes It's Hard to Keep Up

A man knows he has reached mature adulthood when:

He looks forward to a dull evening at home.

The highway patrol look like kids.

His knees buckle and his belt won't.

People start to tell him how young he looks.

A man may not realize how much the midlife transition has changed him until it's over. Life may be radically reoriented—by a decision to prepare for the ministry, start his own business, take up a new hobby or even quit work in support of his wife's career. For others midlife brings little change, which may reflect resignation to a boring job or a positive acceptance of the life structures one has been building. Other men fail to listen to inner voices that question the meaning, value and direction of their lives. For these men, the age fifty transition can be very crisis-producing. Men who have seriously confronted and creatively dealt with the issues raised during their midlife transition seem to sail right through the mature adulthood years.

According to Erikson, the primary developmental task of mature adulthood is *ego integration,* bringing the various parts of one's life structure into a consistent and integrated whole. Men with high ego integration live with a confidence that their life has meaning, value and direction. Men who have shown mastery over the primary developmental task at each stage in their life development are candidates for high ego integration.

For men who were born into an atmosphere of distrust rather than trust, however, life may have been experienced as a series of failures to master the primary task at each developmental stage. Lacking the needed inner resources, these men experience mature adulthood as a state of "ego despair." Due to accumulated strengths or accumulated deficiencies, the lives of men at the mature adulthood stage will vary widely.

There is a *late adult transition* that begins for most men at around age sixty and continues on to retirement, usually around age sixty-five. In this transition men need to conclude the efforts of middle adulthood and prepare for retirement. In this transition men begin to disengage from the situations, relationships and commitments that have held and even driven them during their mature adulthood years. Signs of disengagement include reluctance to make difficult or controversial decisions and pulling away from group and relational involvements that will end at retirement. These men want to retire with a quiet dignity and don't want to do anything that may rock the boat.

Late Adulthood: Time to Be a Boy Again

A man knows he has reached late adulthood when:

He reaches down to straighten his socks and finds he isn't wearing any.

All the names in his little black book end in M.D.

His children begin to look middle-aged.

A little old lady helps him across the street and she's his wife.

For most men, late adulthood begins at retirement, but there is great variety in the degree of life satisfaction men enjoy during this period. For some men, retirement is a difficult adjustment. The workaholic, for instance, is not able to relax and enjoy the fruit of his labor. Others may have tied their life's meaning to busyness, activity and accomplishments. When they can no longer identify an objective accomplishment, they feel unfulfilled. Poor health (one's own or one's wife's) can also sap satisfaction during men's late adulthood. While most older women have developed a network of intimate relationships with family and friends, most men can claim to be intimate only with their wives. The death of a wife can be especially devastating to these men.

For more fortunate men, late adulthood represents the pot of gold at the end of the rainbow. They may have been working hard all their lives, spurred on by the dream of financial security and a leisurely life. This dream can become a reality for men who have mastered their developmental tasks throughout life and who have created a strong and supportive life structure of family and friends.

This vision of masculine maturity, characterized by ego integration and a network of supportive family and friends, is consonant with a biblical view of spiritual maturity. The spiritually mature man will be an empowerer of others. He will seek to invest himself in others, rather than needing others to serve him. At the same time, he is not some isolated "Lone Ranger" trying to do it alone, but serves as part of a caring community. The mature male is able to combine the strengths of separateness and independence within a network of reciprocally caring others.

Such a balance between separateness and connectedness can be seen in the life of the apostle Paul. As Paul was nearing the end of his life, he prepared to pass on the torch to Timothy: "The time of my departure has come. I have fought the good fight, I have finished the race, I have kept the faith" (2 Tim 4:6-7). We would do well to look to Paul as a model of masculine maturity.

PART IV

MEN IN
RELATIONSHIPS

11

FATHERING

Reestablishing the Vital Connection

Boys grow into manhood with a *wounded father* within, a conflicted inner sense of masculinity rooted in men's experience of their fathers as rejecting, incompetent, or absent.

SAMUEL OSHERSON, *FINDING OUR FATHERS*

Søren Kierkegaard tells a wonderful story of how as a young man he was walking down a path with his father when suddenly they came upon a crevasse. Climbing down into it, his father disappeared into the darkness at the bottom. Then he called for his son to jump down and join him. Bewildered, Kierkegaard shouted down to his father, "But I can't see you!" His father shouted back, "Yes, I know, but I can see you."

These words, "But I see you," resonated within the life of Kierkegaard. They reminded him that indeed life is unpredictable and scary; at times one must leap into places and situations that are unknown. Yet he gained solace as he remembered hearing his father's call: "I see you."

Many young boys today long to hear these words from their fathers, but they don't. What they hear instead is, "Don't bother me," "I'm too busy," "Talk to your mother" or, worse yet, silence. This leaves the young boy at the edge of the crevasse with no assurance that he is seen—no assurance that the leap will not destroy him. Tragically, many young men are growing up without a father who will affirm their leap into manhood. As a result, boys reach for manhood with a combination of confusion and fear. Often the voices they do hear are distortions of true manhood.

There is a crisis of fathering today! As we've seen, the roots of the crisis stretch back to the Industrial Revolution and the attendant separation between work and family that removed fathers from the home. The result has been a generation of men who don't know how to father because they have not been fathered themselves.

It is a sad truth that most men today grew up less emotionally bonded with their fathers than any generation of men in the past. Fathers have been able to commit themselves only to a lifetime of hard work and economic support of their family. This has become a part of the ethic of traditional masculinity, which is currently being challenged. Lacking a close relationship with their own fathers, the present generation of fathers are struggling to met the nurturing and emotional needs their children seek.

The void created by the father's absence from the home, although detrimental to both sons and daughters, has proved to have the most adverse effect upon sons. For this reason, I will begin by focusing on the father-son relationship before examining fathering in general. This chapter is an unambiguous plea for a greater commitment to fathering. It is written with the hope that the words "I see you" can again be spoken by fathers to their sons, so that in being seen the sons' sense of self and masculinity can be affirmed.

The Wounded Father Within

The psychological or physical absence of fathers from their families is one of the great underestimated tragedies of our times. In one survey of 7,239 men, almost none said they had been or were close to their fathers, while another found that fewer than two per cent of sons described only good relations with their fathers. In his book on male intimacy, Michael McGill (1985) concludes that the average father is more "phantom man" than "family man." Even when he is present he is absent—there in body, but in every other respect removed from the family.

Present or absent, the father is reliant on his wife to relate to the children on his behalf. Whatever closeness he has with his daughter is more likely to be based on imagery and illusion than on information about himself. His relationship with his son is circumscribed by competition, where "proving oneself is more important than presenting himself."

Reflecting on what a boy can expect to gain from his father, Perry Garfinkel (1985:43) says, "If he has learned well—about the importance of power, achievement, competition, and emotional inexpressiveness—he will enter relationships with other men with great caution and distrust." In his book *Finding Our Fathers: The Unfinished Business of Manhood,* Samuel Osherson describes adult males as have a "wounded father" within, which is the result of experiencing their fathers as cold and distant:

> Men carry around as adults a burden of vulnerability, dependency, or emptiness within themselves, still grieving, reliving a time when going to mother for help as they wanted to was inappropriate, and they wouldn't or couldn't go to father with the confusion, anger, or sadness they felt. When men are put in touch with their pain today, they respond ambivalently—with rage or shame, attempting to prove their independence, as well as with curiosity and a desire to deal with the wounds they feel. (1986:6-7)

Osherson continues, "There is a male vulnerability in relationships that can be traced back to our early childhood experiences of separation and loss. The key to the unfinished business of manhood is unraveling the letting go of our distorted and painful misidentifications with our fathers" (1986:10).

A summary of research on fathering concludes that the traditional emphasis on fathers' being good providers and firm disciplinarians has squeezed out the expectation that they nurture their children (Feldman 1990).

Although much more evidence could be cited to document the inadequacy of fathering in modern society, I believe it's more fruitful to attempt to understand the *reason* for the crisis. In brief, I propose that fathers' being removed from the home after the Industrial Revolution intensified the difficulty males have in the separation-individuation process—the tasks of psychologically separating from their mothers and identifying and bonding with their fathers. To the extent that boys are not succeeding in their struggle, we have a reproduction of *non-fathering*.

The Reproduction of Nonfathering

In her book *The Reproduction of Mothering* (1978), Nancy Chodorow explains why girls grow up to mother—they are merely reproducing behavior they have observed and experienced in relationship with their mothers. An important part of who we are as men, too, is a result of how we were fathered in our formative years. The most important "reproducer" of our manhood is our father. We learn how to be a man, and ultimately how to father, by watching him and experiencing a relationship with him.

Indeed, it is the father who predominantly orients his son to the world from a male perspective. What it is to be a man is mirrored back to the son through the father's actions and words. A son acts out what it means to be a man based upon what he has learned from his father. As he is embraced for these actions, his masculinity is validated and affirmed.

But the reality is that many boys' fathers are physically absent, and thus what is mirrored to them is a distant masculinity. Other fathers are physically present, but since they don't express emotions or communicate about things of the heart, their sons experience them as emotionally absent.

Men who were not validated and affirmed as males in their growing-up years will often be haunted by a fear that they are not man enough. If one were to note how many advertisements use the appeal *Are you man enough?* to goad men into buying a product, one could conclude that this is the major fear among men today. In settings as diverse as the streets of the inner city, the classrooms of colleges and the boardrooms of large corporations, men are propelled by the fear that they are not man enough.

Men who have heard from their fathers, "I see you," are much less driven by the fear of not being man enough. But the sad part is that fathers today were themselves probably deprived of fathers who mirrored manhood to them. As a result, they too are driven by fear, and the sight of their own sons mirrors back to them this fear and confusion. The silence of fathers' voices is echoing forth from generation to generation.

There was a time, before the Industrial Revolution, when most boys grew up seeing and hearing much more of their father. They not only saw him but also worked alongside him, day in and day out. But by the mid-1900s, only ten per cent of American families lived on farms. In most of the other ninety per cent, the mother filled the void created by the father's working outside the home. This is important to understand, because it means that the fathers of most men who are fathers today were more involved in work outside of the home than in nurturing a relationship with them. Mother took over most of the parenting tasks, which had previously been shared with fathers. For the sake of industrial growth, men had been stolen from their homes.

The effect of being reared primarily by a mother is profoundly different for sons and daughters. An abundance of mothering, at the near neglect of fathering, makes girls better prepared than boys to become parents. Boys are at a disadvantage because they grow up lacking nurture from their parent of the same gender. This begins a different process of maturation in boys and girls.

While both boys and girls begin their lives with a primary emotional attachment to their mother, boys must learn to identify with their father by denying attachment to their mother. Girls, on the other hand, can continue to identify with and hold their primary attachment to their mother.

Yet a girl's relationship to her mother is significantly different from a boy's relationship to his father. While the girl is likely to be involved in a face-to-face relationship with her mother in the home, the fact that the father is absent from the home for long periods means that the boy must learn about masculinity from his mother or the culture at large. He doesn't have the advantage of an ongoing personal relationship with his father.

The close ties girls have with their mother will mean they most likely will desire to be nurturing mothers. Since boys are not closely tied to their father, and they deny their attachment to their mother for the sake of their own masculinity, when they in turn become fathers they will likely be emotionally distant from their children.

The effect on marriage will be that these men will struggle to fulfill the emotional needs of their wives. Their wives may well turn to their sons to meet their unfulfilled emotional needs. Trying to avoid becoming substitute husbands to their own mothers, the sons then put up defenses against anything that smacks of femininity. Boys who are parented by mothers more than by fathers, and especially those who have cold and distant relationships with their fathers, will lack nurturing abilities. Boys who experience a non-nurturing father are likely to conform to an exaggerated notion of masculinity. They will compensate for their insecurities by exhibiting an exaggerated form of traditional masculinity. They will appear to be strong, tough, cold, emotionally detached and devoid of nurturing tenderness.

When these patterns are established, the cycle of non-fathering is in place. Although these patterns exist throughout all segments of society, they are especially pronounced in poor families headed by women. Boys who experience a heavy dose of mothering, but lack fathering, seek an affirmation of their masculinity through a male gang. Within the gang, masculinity is proved by being tough, daring and willing to beat up or shoot a rival gang member. The slightest show of sympathy or tenderness can be interpreted as weakness by other gang members. To be cool, detached and void of such "feminine" feelings is to be a real man.

Most men experience a less exaggerated form of psychological constraint. This constraint means that it's easier for most men to participate in rationally oriented roles such as work than in emotionally laden roles such as fathering.

Structural Barriers to Fathering

Not only are there psychological or *internal* constraints upon fathers, keeping them from establishing stronger bonds with their children, but there are also *external* or structural constraints. The relationship between the family and the economy is one example, and the legal system is another.

The fact that the father is usually the main link between the family and the economy means, first, that he is not around the home very much, because his job generally is performed elsewhere. Hence, he has little opportunity to be bonded with his children, even if he wants to be, because his job greatly limits the time he can spend with them. A father must usually crowd any attempts at bonding into a few hours at the end of a workday (when his emotional resources for doing so are probably lowest) or into increasingly busy weekends.

The father may attempt to "telescope" his exchanges with his children into these limited time periods by inventing and improvising shorthand symbols of his love—purchasing gifts, taking the children on a brief excursion after dinner, playing quick-ending games, making jokes and telling bedtime stories. In the process, he runs the risk of becoming little more than an entertainer.

For approximately eight hours a day, the father is in an environment that, by stressing rationality and emotional control rather than emotional expression, tends to reinforce his initial tendencies not to be nurturing.

As mothers are increasingly employed outside of the home, all of this may come to be true of them as well.

Finally, social norms regulating ties between the family and the economy stress the priority of the father's work role, even when this involves hardship for the family. Society expects a mother to give up her job, should it interfere with her relationship to her children, and if the family can possibly do without the income; but the father is expected to give priority to his job over his role as a parent.

By playing down the father-child relationship, the legal system sets up further barriers to the development of deep, meaningful bonding between a father and his children. Fatherhood is not a legally acceptable reason for being deferred from the military draft. Divorce courts usually give the mother custody of the children and relegate the father to the position of a periodic visitor. Fathers can be brought into court for failing to support their children financially, but little is done about the absence of emotional support from fathers.

The blame for weak fathering does not reside only within fathers themselves. To build strong fathering, we must have the conviction and courage to change the social structures that serve as barriers to strong fathering.

Fathering Issues

The psychological and social barriers to fathering described above create several "fathering issues." These include the tendency for fathers more than mothers to engage in sex typing, to assume an instrumental rather than a socioemotional relationship with their children, and to experience conflict with their adolescent children. While some may want to argue that these issues reflect "natural" inborn differences between males and females, research indicates that a father's attachment and bonding behavior is just as strong as a mother's during the first year of a child's life. The decline in attachment and bonding between fathers and their children seems to reflect a response to public expectations more than fathers' personal incompetence.[1]

Sex typing. A familiar nursery rhyme tells us that little girls are made of "sugar and spice and everything nice," but little boys are made of "frogs, snails and puppy-dog tails." This illustrates what is known as sex typing—the practice of making sharp distinctions between male and female characteristics and behavior.

In a survey of more than one thousand parents, parents generally reported that they encouraged sons more than daughters to be competitive, achievement-striving, independent and in control of their feelings, while girls were encouraged to be physically and emotionally expressive (Block 1982). Other studies have found that boys more often than girls were socialized to be dominant (Baumrind 1979), and that girls more often than boys were encouraged to talk about their concerns and feelings and to engage in interpersonal activities (Block 1982; Block, Block and Harrington 1974).

There is evidence that fathers practice sex typing more than mothers, and that they hold to narrower boundaries of sex-appropriate behavior

---

[1]For a fuller discussion of this point, see chapter eight, "The Case for Co-parenting," from Mary Stewart Van Leeuwen's *Gender and Grace* (1990).

for their sons than for their daughters. As an example, fathers of one-year-old boys were very careful to see that their sons learned to play with "male" toys such as cars, trucks and balls. Fathers especially discouraged their sons' playing with dolls.

In a study of parent-adolescent interaction, it was found that the presence of the spouse influenced how much girls and boys were treated differently (Gjerde 1986). For instance, a mother differentiates more between girls and boys in the *presence* of her husband, while a father differentiates more between girls and boys in the *absence* of his wife. It was also found that a father was more responsive and more egalitarian-oriented when he was alone with his son than when his wife was present.

Instrumental responsibilities. An accumulation of research indicates that fathers and mothers relate differently to their children. While fathers tend to assume *instrumental* responsibilities in relationship to their children, mothers tend to assume *socioemotional* responsibilities.

Instrumental responsibilities have to do with guidance parents give their children to enable them to accomplish certain tasks and activities. Examples are helping children learn to dress themselves, tie their own shoes, cross the street, organize homework assignments, ride a bike and, eventually, drive a car. Instrumental parenting also involves attempts to inculcate the right beliefs, values and attitudes in children. It involves teaching children what they must know and how they must behave in order to be in good standing in the family and society.

Socioemotional parenting means attending to children's needs for love, security, nurture and acceptance. This part of parenting involves being sensitive to children's emotional needs, listening to their expression of feelings and expressing feelings to them in return. Whereas instrumental parenting focuses on tasks and context, socioemotional parenting focuses on emotional bonding between parent and child.

The tendency for fathers to interact instrumentally with their children and for mothers to interact socioemotionally begins very early and continues through the child-rearing years. After parents were observed with their children at one month, three months and nine months, one study concluded that mothers were more engaging, response-stimulating, and positively affectionate, while fathers more often engaged in reading and watching television with their infants (Belsky, Gilstrap and Rovine 1984). Another study found that mothers were more likely to hold, tend, display affection toward, smile at and vocalize with their infants than were fathers (Lamb et al. 1982).

Although fathers tend to engage in only instrumental parenting, mothers usually practice both instrumental and socioemotional parenting. Fathers are more restricted in the kind of parenting they practice, and they tend not to become emotionally involved with their children.

When fathers *are* expressive to their children, they tend to express different types of feelings from those that mothers express. Mothers are more likely to express love, tenderness, affection, warmth, happiness, delight, elation, joy, sadness, sorrow and grief to their children; fathers are more likely to express anger, hate, rage and resentment. This difference between fathers and mothers is true whether the feelings are expressed verbally or physically.

Needless to say, these differences correspond to traditional gender-role stereotypes that define certain feelings as appropriate for females and others as appropriate for males. The effect of these differences upon children is obvious, since much of what children learn is "caught" and not taught. In growing up, sons see their mothers model the expression of feelings like love, happiness and sadness, and they see their fathers model angry feelings. Boys come to "reproduce" the "manly" feelings, while holding back on the feelings that seem to be exhibited only by females.

Conflict with adolescent children. The previous chapter discussed the stressful aspects of being a male at each life-cycle stage. As it happens, most fathers experience their midlife transition *at the same time* that their children are in adolescence. Since both adolescents and middle-aged parents are struggling with identity issues, fathering adolescents is particularly challenging. A middle-aged father and a teenage son can constitute a double inferiority complex, because both are likely to feel insecure about who they are.

In establishing their own identity, adolescents need to exert independence. Fathers who feel good about themselves can accept this; they won't be threatened by what they see as a passing need in their children.

Fathers who, on the other hand, are experiencing their own identity crisis will not be as psychologically prepared to handle rejection from their children.

The converse is also true. A father undergoing a midlife crisis may have personal needs that will put demands on his relationship with his children. The child who has already established a clear sense of self and is not in the midst of an identity crisis is in a better position to be supportive of the needy parent.

Another factor in father-son conflicts is that midlife fathers and adolescent sons are experiencing opposite physiological changes. Just as the son is beginning to develop the physical characteristics of adulthood, the father may begin to lose his. While the adolescent boy finds his muscles growing and his physical strength increasing, the father finds his muscles shrinking and his strength declining.

I recall teaching my son to play tennis when he was ten years old. By the time he had reached sixteen, we were quite evenly matched. When Joel was eighteen and I was in my mid-forties, my worst nightmare came true: he consistently beat me. There were times when my competitive spirit, unable to mobilize my body to live up to my expectations, made it difficult for me to be a gracious loser.

Fathering adolescent children is also likely to be problematic because issues of authority are likely to intensify. Adolescents' main task in relation to both their parents is differentiation. Differentiation is simply the process of separating from one's parents. Adolescents have the psychological task of becoming their own person by embracing or letting go of their parents' attitudes, beliefs and values.

Fathers can be detrimental to the healthy differentiation of their adolescent children if they respond by being either too *restrictive* or too *permissive*. Either of these extremes is likely to exacerbate issues of control and independence.

Adolescents struggle against being controlled by their parents—they want independence. The transition from dependence to independence takes place most smoothly in homes where fathers have created a flexible yet structured environment. Highly restrictive fathers, who hold the reins too tightly, create rigid structures in which there is little flexibility. Under these circumstances, the adolescent child feels frustrated and seeks independence by rebelling against the father's rigid authority.

At the opposite extreme, children of highly permissive fathers can become frustrated and confused because they don't know what the rules are. Extremely permissive fathers not only allow their children to make basic decisions but also fail to set limits for their behavior. When fathers are silent and do not clearly state rules and limits, children generally respond to the ambiguity by behaving in more and more extreme ways in an attempt to discover precisely what the rules and limits are.

Suppose a son goes to his father and asks, "Dad, how late can I stay out tonight?" His father says, "Use your own judgment; just don't stay out too late." The son comes home at 2:00 a.m., and the father is furious because the son stayed out "too late."

The next Saturday night, the son inquires again, "Dad, how late can I stay out?" Again the father replies, "Use your judgment, but don't stay out too late." The son comes home at 1:00 a.m., and the father is again angry. This goes on until the son "discovers" the unspoken rule that the father has refused to communicate clearly.

Teenage children have a great need to know what the rules are, even when they may not agree with those rules. Not only are they frustrated when a father does not give clear rules, but they may also interpret silence as a lack of interest. Having reached such a conclusion, a teenager may rebel as a way to gain his father's attention.

Fathering daughters. The strong focus in this chapter on the father-son relationship is not meant to slight the importance of fathering to the development of daughters. Fathers seem to be especially important in contributing to the healthy development of their daughters' sense of self and feminine identity. Where the father-daughter relationship is weak, the daughter is more likely to be enmeshed (too united) with her mother. A strong relationship with the father facilitates a daughter's differentiating from her mother and establishing her own sense of boundaries. Daughters are best able to develop a separate sense of self when they are securely related to both of their parents.

By affirming his daughter, a father can contribute to her strong sense of independence and self-confidence—and these in turn will allow her to behave with confidence. In a study of successful women in male-dominated professions, it was found that the one thing most of these women had in common was a highly affirming and supportive father. What began as a perception of their fathers' confidence in them became internalized into a *self*-confidence, which resulted in succeeding where many other women had failed.

Daughters' feminine identity is also based upon healthy, affirming relationships with their fathers. The daughter whose father tells her that she is capable, pleasant and attractive will come to see herself as sufficiently feminine. Daughters who do not feel that their femininity is affirmed by their fathers are more likely to be unsure of themselves in relating to other males.

The way a father relates to his daughter sets the tone for the way she will relate to men. The daughter whose father is sexually abusive, or who makes sexually suggestive remarks, is likely to struggle when attempting to establish trusting relationships with men. Having experienced a violation of her personal boundaries, she will be on guard against similar intrusions. A daughter who has experienced a safe, secure and affirming relationship with her father is better prepared to develop healthy relationships with men.

Fathers are more able to physically demonstrate their love and affection for their daughters than for their sons. As the daughter begins to mature physically, however, the father can become uncomfortable about showing his feelings. In a scene from the TV series "All in the Family," Archie Bunker's daughter, Gloria, has been dangerously ill. Archie walks into the room where she lies in apparent unconsciousness. He begins telling her how much she means to him, how much he loves her. But she has been pretending, and suddenly she sits up and exclaims, "It's so great to hear you say it, Daddy!" Archie, instead of taking his child in his arms, snorts disgustedly and shakes her off.

Probably Archie reacts as if he had been caught doing something wrong because he doesn't know how to handle his feelings of attraction for his daughter. And yet it is precisely during their teenage years that daughters most need to be affirmed by their fathers.

A Biblical Model of Fathering

A biblical model of fathering can best be derived from the scriptural depiction of God as Father.[2] A good one-word description of God's fathering is *love*. Myron Chartier (1987) has observed that God displays his fathering love in seven ways.

First, God cares for people. Although this is preeminently demonstrated in the incarnation, death and resurrection of Christ, numerous other biblical passages stress God's caring nature (for example, Lk 15:11-32; 1 Pet 5:7).

Second, God is responsive to human needs. This can be seen in the covenant that was established after the flood (Gen 9:8-17), in the rescue of Israel from Egypt and in Jesus' free offer of mercy and restoration (Jn 3:16; Tit 3:3-7).

Third, God bestows rich gifts on us—the only begotten Son and the Holy Spirit as Comforter.

Fourth, God shows respect for, values and cherishes us; there is no attempt to dominate, and we are given the freedom to be ourselves.

Fifth, God knows us, for Jesus came in human likeness (Jn 1:14; Phil 2:5-8; Heb 2:17-18; 4:15); this is a knowledge that penetrates to the core of our existence (Ps 44:21; Jn 2:24-25).

Sixth, God forgives (Mt 26:28; Jn 3:16-17; Eph 1:7).

Seventh, God disciplines us (Prov 3:11-12; Heb 12:5-8; Rev 3:19). The discipline of Israel can be seen as an attempt to create a faithful and obedient people.

Clearly, the biblical emphasis is on the love and grace God so freely gives. The first six points above, taken together, express *covenant love,* God's unconditional love for us his children. Yet this unconditional love is not free of expectations and demands. Thus, as the seventh point shows, God's love includes disciplinary action for our good. His love as Father bears a striking similarity to the parenting style advocated in

---

[2]These scriptural references can be used to build a biblical model of *parenting* (equally valid for mothering *and* fathering), but they are still specifically relevant to fathering. See Jack and Judy Balswick, *The Family: A Christian Perspective on the Home* (Grand Rapids, Mich.: Baker, 1990).

the social science literature: *a high degree of support and inductive control (using logic and reasoning) rather than coercive control (using force)* (Baumrind 1967, 1979; Rollins and Thomas 1979). The actions of God as Father clearly point to a model in which father love (support) and discipline (control) intertwine to help children develop toward maturity.

All that I said in chapter seven on Christian empowering is also applicable to Christian fathering. Fathers are in a position of power over their children. But like our heavenly Father, we are to use our power to empower our children from dependence to maturity. In this sense, fathering can be seen as discipling. Christian fathering is the process of instilling confidence, of strengthening and building children up to become more powerful and competent. The model Scripture presents of God in relationship to his children is one of *strong fathering*—caring, responsive, giving, respecting, knowing, forgiving and disciplining.

Those who argue that mothering is more important than fathering will not find support in Scripture. In fact, if one were to take literally what the Bible says about God as Father, one could argue that fathering is *more* important than mothering.

At present most parenting is, in reality, mothering. My appeal is not for strong fathering to replace strong mothering, but rather that the two should go hand in hand. Recent evidence suggests that there are a growing number of "latchkey children" who are deprived of both strong mothering and strong fathering.

When father and mother are jointly involved in parenting, a family has what family therapists refer to as a strong "parental subsystem." The ideal model, from a biblical and a social science perspective, is *coparenting*.

In her important book *Gender and Grace* (1990), Mary Stewart Van Leeuwen devotes a whole chapter to evidence supporting a coparenting model. Diane Ehrensaft's book *Parenting Together: Men and Women Sharing the Care of Their Children* (1990) gives further conclusive evidence of the benefit of coparenting. Among other things, Ehrensaft reports that coparented children, compared to those who had not been coparented, (1) had a more secure sense of basic trust, (2) more successfully adapted to brief separations from the mother, (3) had closer relationships to both mother and father, (4) developed better social discrimination skills, such as discerning who can best meet their needs, (5) displayed greater creativity and moral development, (6) had less animosity toward the other gender, (7) were better able to develop strong friendship bonds with opposite-gender children and (8) displayed fantasies of sustained connectedness.

As one might expect, sons reaped the greatest benefits from coparenting. Sons who had strong bonds with both their fathers and their mothers were more able to display empathy, affection and nurturing behavior; thought highly of the way they were parented; and were more likely to state that they wanted to "be a father" when they grew up. Girls who were coparented showed a greater sense of self and clearer personal boundaries.

The only "risk" reported in the coparenting literature is the possibility that two highly involved parents might "overstimulate" or give excessive attention to their children, which could result in inhibiting children's ability to be creative and figure things out for themselves. But there were few reported cases of this problem. Given the current evidence of child neglect by both mothers and fathers, overparenting would seem to be a most welcome "problem."

There is also abundant evidence that coparenting is a benefit to parents. Among the benefits of coparenting to parents are that (1) mothers are less likely to be enmeshed or overinvolved with their children, (2) working mothers have some relief from what in reality is often two jobs—one in the economic force and one at home, (3) parenting decisions are made on the basis of both parents' understanding of, and involvement with, their children, (4) discipline of children is more consistent and effective, (5) fathers are more in touch with their feelings and more able to express them and (6) fathers are more nurturing and sensitive in their relationships with others.

A Fuller Manhood: The Fruit of Strong Fathering

Children need and desire strong fathering. Many children sense that Mother is really in charge, because Dad either is not interested or is too busy to pay much attention to them. Strong fathering will not only benefit children but also yield great dividends to mothers and fathers.

One of mothers' greatest frustrations is that their husbands do not take a more active role in parenting. While it's true that some mothers allow themselves to get trapped into a codependent relationship with their children, most would be more than willing for their husbands to become more involved in parenting. Mothers are more likely to become codependent with their children when they are in a weak relationship with their husbands. For example, the wife who is not receiving emotional fulfillment from her husband may seek this from her children—and may panic when her children begin to seek an emotional relationship elsewhere.

Fathers who spend little time with their children are likely to argue that it's the quality and not the quantity of time they spend with their children that counts. However, research shows that *both* quantity and quality of time are important. In fact, the two are related—those fathers who spend quality time with their children are also the ones who spend longer periods of time.

Time with children cannot be rushed. The process (quantity) as well as the content (quality) of fathering is important. In and of itself, the act of taking time away from a busy life can have a most positive effect upon a child.

Strong fathering can do more than anything else to build strong, confident masculinity. Fathers who become involved in the parenting process will develop their socioemotional and relational sides. In contrast to the world of work outside the home, where decisions are expected to be based on reason and logic rather than emotion, taking care of children inclines men to consider personal and emotional issues. This will not only change men in the home but can have a positive impact on the way they perform their work as well. Men who have high empathy skills can more effectively relate to the people they must work with daily. Even management theory now stresses the need for personnel in the business world to understand the social and emotional needs of workers.

Finally, strong fathering can have a profound positive effect on how boys develop. Boys who grow up with a strong relationship with their fathers can become men who are both strong and nurturing, rational and emotional, hard and soft. They can be the kind of fathers we all wish we'd had.

My Own Story

For ten years I was privileged to have a son who was warm, loving and expressive of his feelings. Jeff died a few days short of his tenth birthday, after a three-month fight with cancer.

My warmest memories of Jeff are the times when we enjoyed intimacy. A bedtime ritual I established with him was to tuck him in bed and, before turning off the light, tell him that I loved him. He would invariably reply, "I love you too, Dad." Sometimes he even beat me to the punch and said, "I love you, Dad," before I had a chance to express my love to him.

But our relationship hadn't always been so close. Until four years earlier, I had devoted so much time to surviving as a beginning assistant professor at the university that I had little quality time left over for fathering.

The change came when Judy, my wife, began to work on her doctoral degree. I had to be home at 2:30 each afternoon to meet the kids when they got off the school bus, help them with their homework, fix dinner and in general become more than a part-time father. As I look back now, I truly consider this change a blessing in disguise. For if any circumstance made the dying of my son more bearable, it was that over the four years before his death Jeff and I became intimate friends.

One evening, lying on the living-room sofa that had been his bed for a month, Jeff suddenly said to Judy, "Mom, I'm going to die!"

"I know, Jeff," Judy said. "Is that okay?"

"How long will it take?" Jeff asked.

"Do you mean until you die, or until you get to heaven?" we asked. Throughout the illness, Jeff had been very aware of his closeness to God and totally secure in the love of Jesus Christ as his Savior.

"To heaven," he answered.

I assured him that when he died he would be with God immediately. We sensed that this would be the last evening we would share as a family. That night Jeff died peacefully in his sleep.

A few days after Jeff's death, we were cleaning out his dresser drawers and found a note he had written to us sometime in the past. The note read, "I love you, Mom and Dad, even when you get mad at me. I will always love you."

As I reflected on the closeness of our relationship, I thanked God for using circumstances to develop me beyond the shallow father I had been into one who could say, "I love you, Son," anticipating the delight of hearing "I love you, Dad," in return.

12
MALE FRIENDSHIPS
Finding Our Brothers

If he has learned well—about the importance of power, achievement, competition, and emotional inexpressive-ness—he will enter relationships with other men with great caution and distrust.

PERRY GARFINKEL, *IN A MAN'S WORLD*

At a recent men's retreat, a man in his forties made this confession to me: "When I observe my wife, I notice that she seems to be involved at a deeper level with her female friends than I am with my male friends. I have also noticed that when her friends move away she regularly keeps in touch with them. With me, I seem to take my friendships for granted, I seldom write or telephone a male friend unless I have good reason to do so. I sometimes think something is missing in my friendship with other men."

If we are honest, more than a few of us males identify with this. We have a nagging feeling that something's missing in our male friendships, an observation that is supported in social science literature. According to *The McGill Report on Male Intimacy,* male friendships are "superficial, even shallow." Even the best of buddies "reveal so little of themselves to each other that they are little more than acquaintances. There is no intimacy in most male relationships and none in what intimacy offers: solace and support" (McGill 1985:184). In his book *In a Man's World: Father, Son, Brother, Friend and Other Roles Men Play,* Perry Garfinkel observes that men may join clubs to retreat from the competitive, non-nurturing society at large, but "once inside . . . they are faced with similar struggles and competitions for power and control. . . . A man comes away from his men's club and fraternity experience with mixed feelings. His need to belong is fulfilled but his need for closeness to men may not be" (Garfinkel 1985:107). Although Garfinkel finds a lack of intimacy among men, he believes they should not be content in this condition: "Men should talk to each other. Not the proverbial 'shoptalk,' but the deeper feelings about work, about love, about themselves, *about their feelings for each other*" (1985:180).

In earlier chapters, we learned that while women are inclined toward connectedness, men are inclined toward separateness. These gender-based tendencies may result in barriers to the development of intimacy between men. After considering these barriers in the first part of the chapter, I will suggest that they may merely encourage men to develop *alternative* styles of relating to each other. It may be that a female style of intimacy has come to be accepted as normative, while an equally legitimate male intimacy style has been ignored. The chapter will end by suggesting ways in which male friendships can better fulfill men's relational needs.

Barriers to Male Friendships

Men are less able to relate in an open, verbally expressive way to each other than are women. There are two aspects of the traditional male role that are primarily responsible for this: *competition,* which was discussed in the previous chapter, and *homophobia.*

Homophobia. A real man is known not only by what he does but also by what he does not do. Above all, a man must not appear to be too feminine—to act like a woman. Related to men's fear of femininity is their fear of closeness with another man. This fear of closeness among men is known as *homophobia.*

Homophobia begins in the home. This is to say that the source of men's fear of closeness with other men can be found in the relationships their parents established with them as children. As I noted earlier, where the mother is the primary caretaker, children develop a stronger emotional attachment to her than to their father, and this affects boys differently than girls. In establishing an opposite-gender identity, a boy must try to decrease his dependence upon his mother and increasingly separate from her in a way that his sister need not do. An important psychological difference between males and females stems from the fact that while girls work out their female identity while connected to their same-gender parent, boys must work out their masculine identity *disconnected* from their same-gender parent.

Children's sense of self is most strongly affected by their most strongly bonded relationship. For a girl, the parent with whom she has the strongest emotional bond is also the one who serves as a female role model. For the boy, however, the parent with whom he has the strongest emotional bond cannot provide a masculine role model. For the father is likely to be both physically and emotionally absent from the home for long periods of time. So the boy has to learn masculinity from his mother and the culture at large.

The result is that the boy grows up with less capacity for empathy than his sister does. While the girl has a basis for experiencing another's needs or feelings as her own, the boy's identity must be defined partly in terms of *denial* of the close, dependent bonding he experienced with his mother. In order for the boy to feel adequately masculine, he must distinguish and differentiate himself from anything considered feminine. By the time the boy reaches adulthood, he has learned to define his masculinity negatively—as that which is *not* feminine. He becomes skilled in repressing and denying his gentle, nurturing side.

Fear of femininity and homophobia are similar fears in that both have to do with the male's need to affirm his masculinity. The fear of femininity is central to understanding homophobia, because homosexuality, femininity and effeminate demeanor are all wrapped up together in a complex of male fears. Note the common insults young boys hurl at each other—pansy, fag, panty-waist, girlie boy, homo, fem. A man fears becoming too emotionally close to another man because others might conclude that he is feminine, effeminate or even homosexual.

Generally, the more secure a man is in his sexuality, the more open he can be in relating to another man. The man who is secure in his masculinity can put his arms around another man or verbally express his affection to him.

In his novel *P.S., Your Cat Is Dead!* James Kirkwood captures the essence of male "skin hunger" in an interchange between two male characters:

One evening about three months into our friendship, after we'd taken our dates home, we stopped by a bar for a nightcap. We ended by having three or four and when we left and were walking down the street, Pete suddenly slipped his arm around my shoulder. He surprised me; there was extreme warmth and intimacy about the gesture. When I looked over at him, he grinned and said, "That bother you?"

"No . . . ," I shrugged in return.

He then gave my shoulder a squeeze. "Ever since I've known you, you got me pretending I don't have arms." (Kirkwood 1973:23)

Compared to other cultures of the world, Western males are very undemonstrative and inhibited about showing love to each other. In many cultures, open touching between two male friends is an expression of affection with no homosexual overtones.

As I related earlier in this book, in Cyprus I had the opportunity to observe relationships between male friends of another culture. I noticed how easily Greek Cypriot males expressed their affection for each other. They danced with each other and were free to tell each other what they were feeling. At first this made me feel uncomfortable, as it contrasted so sharply with the way American males usually disguise their feelings of affection for each other.

A few years later, when studying and traveling in India, I became close to an Indian man who was my companion for the entire summer. One afternoon we were traveling by public bus in New Delhi and were engaged in deep conversation. Suddenly I realized that my friend, Rajgopal, was holding my hand as we talked. I felt quite embarrassed until I looked around and remembered where I was. No one on the bus was staring at us in disbelief. No one seemed to feel that we were doing something wrong. No one suggested that there was anything unusual about the physical expression of our friendship. In India it was often expected that male friends would hold hands or put their arms around each other as they talked.

Homophobia is clearly limiting to men, because it makes emotional intimacy with another man difficult. When this fact is coupled with the finding that men are more likely than women to perceive the world in sexual terms, make sexual judgments and attribute sexual meaning and intent to a "friendly" situation, we have a clearer understanding of the confusion between intimacy and sexual behavior.

Homophobia is a major barrier to close male-to-male relationships, restricts us to very narrowly defined, rigid friendships that do not allow for emotional closeness or a sharing of feelings. Homophobia is a powerful force to prevent male friendships from developing emotional depth.

Conboys: Institutionalized competition. In the previous chapter I concluded that competition between men creates an atmosphere of suspicion. This suspiciousness between men has been institutionalized in the development of the *conboy* role. Webster defines "con" as a swindler, or one who attempts to direct the course of another. Unfortunately, this is a good description of one way a man can relate to another man.

The conboy role includes the types of manipulative behavior we associate with the "con man," "con artist" or "wheeler-dealer." I purposefully refer to this type as a con*boy* to connote that this type of behavior is less than mature; it should not be dignified by being attributed to *men.* The conboy becomes a skilled manipulator of other males through his ability to convince them he really likes and cares for them.

Certain occupational roles, such as the traveling salesman, carry the stereotypical expectations of conboy behavior. To the extent that the techniques of selling involve flattering and ego-building of a would-be client, the salesman is playing the role of a conboy. In the competitive structure of much of the workaday world, males have learned to be on guard against such manipulative behavior in other males.

The conboy's attempts at manipulation may even be ethically justified within certain male subcultures. The conboy learns to rationalize his manipulation of other men by believing that the "sucker," or naive "mark," deserves to be taken advantage of. The skilled conboy may even achieve status within his subculture because of his reputation as a skilled manipulator. The conboy role has become institutionalized in some sales meetings, where salesmen share stories on the types of manipulative behavior that work best with clients. Conboys easily identify and uphold W. C. Fields's famous line, "Never give a sucker an even break."

The ethics and philosophy of the conboy role are modified from those of the rugged frontier individualist who makes it to the top on his own. Instead of succeeding "the old-fashioned way"—by hard work, self-discipline and honesty—the conboy models his behavior upon the equally hard-working folk hero who schemed, connived and sometimes "clawed" his way to the top.

Given that many men report they feel suspicious of other men and have a difficult time trusting them, it seems that the conboy role is all too commonly adopted in our society. I recently saw a man wearing a T-shirt that would be a perfect epitaph for the conboy—"Whoever dies with the most toys wins!"

Male Friendship Structures

Although homophobia and competition can hinder the development of open, sharing relationships between men, they do not altogether prevent the development of meaningful male friendships. The types of friendships men develop with each other, however, may reflect the nature of these barriers. Men form their friendships in a way that protects them from appearing less than fully masculine and keeps them from appearing to compete with each other.

I've identified four general types of male friendships—*Good Ol' Boys, Locker-Room Boys, Sidekicks-Topkicks* and *Mentors-Novices*. While the first two friendship structures in part serve to protect men from their homophobia and to keep outsiders out, the last two types are hierarchically structured to protect men from competing with each other.

Good Ol' Boys. "Good ol' boy" is primarily a Southern expression, coined by the flamboyant Louisiana governor Huey Long. The term was popularized through the mass media's interest in President Jimmy Carter's brother, Billy Carter. Billy and his male friends who sat in the service station drinking beer and swapping stories were good ol' boys to each other.

Good ol' boy relationships do not arise overnight; rather, they often begin during childhood and are nurtured through the trials and triumphs of growing up together. The good ol' boy is completely loyal to the other good ol' boys, who together form a strong in-group. A good ol' boy can be counted on during a time of trouble or need, for he will stick with a buddy "through thick and thin."

Although good ol' boys spend much time talking together, they rarely communicate their personal feelings to each other. If asked why he doesn't talk about his feelings, the good ol' boy is likely to reply that it isn't necessary, because his buddies know what he's thinking without having to ask him. He may also say, "Man, if you have to say it, the feelings must not be there."

He considers expressing feelings a "womanly" thing to do. The man who is expressive of his feelings is likely to be laughed at and joked about by the good ol' boys as one who is "too feminine" or lacks "manliness." Good ol' boys do have deep, sincere, enduring feelings for each other demonstrated in the supportive *action* they will take on each other's behalf.

Good ol' boy roles are both fostered by and perpetuators of a powerful male subculture. This subculture is a storehouse of folk philosophy, humor, wisdom and stereotypes transmitted to males as they begin to learn the good ol' boy role. By the time adulthood is reached, each good ol' boy shares in the memories, stories and wisdom that make lengthy conversation unnecessary. A brief statement or comment can conjure up a common memory in the good ol' boys group, drawing a collective laugh or another response and then leading the group to another shared memory.

It's difficult, if not impossible, for a woman to become a part of this subculture. It's also hard for a male who does not share the good ol' boys' heritage.

Good ol' boy friendships can be extremely meaningful and supportive to men. Yet they may be lacking a vital emotionally expressive component in crisis situations. Take the case of a man who has just found out that his young son has terminal cancer and is given four months to live. While the hurting father may need verbal expressions of caring and empathy, the good ol' boy may only be capable of an uncomfortable silence; or he may clumsily try to distract attention from the obvious hurt his friend is feeling.

Good ol' boys have even more difficulty in communicating to someone outside their group. They often leave this job to their wives. Women have ways of expressing care and support to families or friends in crisis—bringing food, sending flowers, starting a prayer chain and the like. Men, it seems, leave this crisis work to women, because they haven't worked out comfortable ways to express support to friends in times of emotional need. While the good ol' boy may communicate feelings to his buddies in nonverbal ways, outsiders who are not privy to these shared nonverbal codes may find it impossible to detect such communication.

I believe that most men are good ol' boys to a certain extent. Good ol' boy types of behavior transcend most social, class, geographical and ethnic boundaries. Every time men "go out with the guys" to a ball game or to hunt or fish, they are likely to engage in good ol' boy behavior.

Locker-Room Boys. Something happens to men under the emotional pressures of cooperating to reach a difficult goal. In the process, they can achieve a degree of emotional sharing that is not characteristic of good ol' boys. They become emotionally open to each other in ways they are not with women.

In a certain way most males feel more comfortable around men than women—that is, in the security of a male subculture. The locker-room boy is dependent upon such "masculine" subcultures as men's athletic clubs, sports teams, bars, military combat and gaming rooms. In these environments, where masculine identity is secure, the locker-room boy is better able to express his gentle, affectionate feelings.

Locker-room friendships transcend the boundaries of social stratification. After a few beers at the neighborhood tavern, men who have spent the day working in a factory will begin to share their feelings and concerns with each other. Such emotional sharing does not take place between them and their wives.

Football players will enthusiastically hug each other after a touchdown. In the locker room, they will openly weep or express affection for each other after a victory or defeat. After losing the 1976 World Series, the New York Yankees' fiery manager, Billy Martin, announced to the media that he *loved* his ball players. The next year the Yankees won the World Series, and the televised after-game celebration showed Billy Martin and the series hero, Reggie Jackson, with their arms around each other. Although they had been feuding the entire season, Reggie said, "I love you, Billy," and Billy replied, "I love you too, Reggie." In the security of the locker room, such expressions of affection were accepted as completely normal.

Since the athlete's masculinity has been established through his physical prowess, he is free to express his feelings without having his masculinity questioned. The locker-room boy is able to share his feelings with certain other men in "masculine" environments.

Any male who has participated in male sports knows that much locker-room bantering actually disguises closeness and affection. Three times a week I play volleyball with a group of men at our local YMCA. When I began playing with them ten years ago, I noticed that they shot brutal verbal put-downs at each other. There were attacks on a man's masculinity ("That was a wimpy hit; why aren't you playing with the women?") attacks on age ("Why don't you go home and return tomorrow afternoon—that's when the class for elderly basket-weaving meets") and attacks on physical mobility ("Hit the ball in front of the statue").

Since I was a newcomer, the men did not aim any of these put-downs at me. As I came to be accepted into the group, however, I too became a target. And after ten years, I know who my closest friends are on the volleyball court—the ones who put me down the *most.* Men who are in conflict, or unsure of their relationship, do not verbally put each other down, because their relationship lacks the necessary security.

Maybe I'm too much a part of the locker-room boy subculture, but I think these put-downs should be accepted for what they are: code words for closeness and affection. They are certainly not abusive words, although an outsider might assume that they are. But it's unfortunate that men can't express their feelings more openly to each other; we need to be open to a healthier "masculine" mode of building one another up through friendship.

When I taught at the University of Georgia, I was part of a YMCA men's volleyball team. One of my teammates, who was forty-one years old at the time, died from a heart attack on the playing court. The depth of the friendship between team members was verified by the fact that all of us selected to be pallbearers at Karl's funeral were from the volleyball team. Our open weeping as we carried Karl's body down the church aisle into the waiting hearse revealed in public the depth of the love we'd developed for our friend. Although I think Karl knew it, I still regret that he died without my having told him how much I valued our friendship.

Sidekicks-Topkicks. The Lone Ranger and Tonto, Batman and Robin, the Cisco Kid and Poncho, Sherlock Holmes and Watson—these are all examples of devoted male friendships that are hierarchical. Tonto, Robin, Poncho and Watson are all "sidekicks" to the Lone Ranger, Batman, the Cisco Kid and Sherlock Holmes, respectively, who are "topkicks."

In each of these relationships one man is clearly the superior. The inequalities are based upon differences in personal qualities. In each case, the topkick is the leader due to his superiority in strength, wisdom, knowledge, experience, skill or some other valued quality. Both the sidekick and the topkick recognize this inequality. Each is invaluable to the other, but in a different way. The topkick leads, and the sidekick loyally follows. The sidekick will offer suggestions, but his primary function is to serve as a sounding board to the topkick.

When the topkick is absent or indisposed, the sidekick may assume the role of leadership. This is an opportunity for the sidekick to prove his loyalty and capabilities. When the Long Ranger has been shot, we know that Tonto will take over. When Batman is being held captive, we know that Robin will prove his worth by directing a rescue mission. It is almost as if the topkick needs to be incapacitated *before* the sidekick can or will ascend to the leadership role. When the topkick returns, note how the sidekick returns to his designated role *alongside* the topkick.

Sidekicks and topkicks are equal in the sense that each would risk his life for the sake of the other. There is a deep trust and loyalty between the two friends. In power and leadership, however, the two are not equal. The topkick is clearly in charge, and this functions to keep the relationship from becoming a competitive one.

As I mentioned earlier, men have difficulty handling intimacy between each other. In a relationship of devotion between two men, there may be a fear of intimacy, and a fear that the relationship will have homosexual overtones. The sidekick-topkick relationship is one way men solve the difficulty they have with both competition and intimacy.

One is hard put to find examples of female buddy friendships in either the traditional literature or the popular media. Those that do exist do not seem to be built on the hierarchical topkick-sidekick model. Female friendships tend to be more equal and to allow for a greater degree of intimacy than male relationships. This is exemplified in one of the few female buddy relationships to be depicted in a television series—"Cagney and Lacey." While Lacey's formal rank was slightly above Cagney's, the relationship had an egalitarian tone. In fact, the inequality in rank was often highlighted as incongruent to the assumed equality between the two women police officers.

The 1991 film *Thelma and Louise* gained much media attention because it depicted two women engaging in the type of devil-may-care behavior that had always been exclusive to male buddy films. But even here, it is difficult to differentiate Thelma and Louise into a topkick-sidekick hierarchy.

Mentors-Novices. The mentor-novice relationship is a hierarchy based upon an inequality of knowledge or skill that usually reflects a difference in age. The mentor is older and wiser and has a higher position in the relationship because he has achieved a status to which the novice aspires. At the very minimum, the mentor passes on his knowledge and wisdom to the novice. In the fullest, most effective mentoring relationship, the mentor also assumes responsibility for the novice's development and well-being.

It's worth noting that within the German graduate educational system a mentor is called a *doctor-father,* while within the Dutch system a mentor is one's *promoter.* In the German system the mentor becomes like a father—demanding respect, to be sure, but nevertheless reliable as one who will watch out for the student in a fatherly way. In the Dutch system, the mentor is the promoter of the student's *total* welfare.

In most societies throughout history, younger men have been mentored by men who are older and more experienced. These older men assumed responsibility for the younger men and invested their knowledge and wisdom into them. The poet Robert Bly is right when, in his popular book *Iron John* (1990), he decries the lack of male mentoring in contemporary industrial societies. Young men need mentors, but many older men are incapable of offering this because they themselves were not mentored. The inaccessibility of older men has caused younger men to mistrust them. The cry of males growing up in the 1960s was "Never trust anyone over thirty." Bly observes that these young men pointed out that it was older men, the government decision-makers, who sent young men to be slaughtered in meaningless battles in the jungles of Vietnam.

What little mentoring does take place in modern society is often done by males who are only a little older than those they are attempting to mentor. For example, the major mentors for the fatherless boys living in our urban ghettos are older teenage gang leaders. Most of these boys have not experienced a relationship with any adult male who is old enough to be their father. Those who do have contact with their father are more likely to experience him as uninterested and unsupportive. Although not as emotionally deprived as boys in urban ghettos, many middle-class boys also suffer from an absence of a close father-son relationship.

That males tend to define their friendships with each other on the basis of hierarchy should not surprise us. A result of the curse described in Genesis 3 is not only that men will attempt to lord it over women, but that they will also try to lord it over each other. The attempt to be in a superior position may be one of the greatest hindrances to men's being able to *care* for each other.

But this reality should not negate the necessity of mentor-novice friendships. We need more of them rather than fewer. But we need to find ways to bring gentleness into the mentoring friendship. It needs to be a place for openness and "emotional holding" between younger males and older males. The mentor-novice friendship must allow younger males to share their fears and anxieties without wondering whether the older males will reject them. The mentor, in return, needs to feel secure enough to share his own fears and difficulties as the novice matures. The ideal mentor-novice friendship should culminate in a mutually empowering relationship, as described in chapter seven.

Nurture: The Missing Ingredient

I believe that males have intimacy styles that are legitimate alternatives to female intimacy styles. I've suggested that each of the four types of male friendships listed above—good ol' boys, locker-room boys, top-kick-sidekicks and mentor-novices—is formed in response to the difficulties men have with intimacy and competition. These are not "bad" types of friendships; there is much that is commendable within each. Yet each contains built-in barriers restricting men from meeting the whole range of their friendship needs. Male friendships need to be expanded to include nurture and caretaking.

Men have traditionally felt more comfortable assuming a caretaking role with females than with other males. This is partly based on the assumption that, because males are stronger than females, it is men's duty to protect women. But men find it difficult to care for dependent younger males (young children) and dependent older males (their aging fathers). It seems that men are uncomfortable offering nurture to other males. Men need to learn to be caretakers to males who need nurturing.

In the previous chapter I stressed that fathers need to develop strong emotional bonds with their sons while they are still young. Here I will add only that men are needed, and need themselves, to be involved in nurturing relationships with younger males. Infants need to experience being held and cuddled by men, not just by women. Young children need to mature with the realization that tenderness and love are available from men. Children need to know that they can expect to be comforted by a man when they cry. Children need to experience the combination of strength and tenderness that is a part of masculine caretaking.

And men themselves need to experience what nurturing a small child can give them. The man who holds and caresses a baby in his arms, feeling the smoothness and warmth of its skin and hearing its soft cooing, becomes a different person. The best way for men to become nurturing people is to nurture. Out of the nurturing experiences men will become more nurturing.

Older men also need nurturing and caretaking from other men and not just from women. A grown man needs to learn to nurture his father and other older male friends. But it's not only the very young and very old who are in need of caretaking. Men of all ages need nurture, and they need to experience some of it from other men!

Jesus: A nurturing caretaker. In his relationship with his disciples Jesus was the model nurturer. Jesus' friendships included both an *active doing* dimension and a *confiding intimacy* dimension. John records that Jesus said to his disciples, "No one has greater love than this, to lay down one's life for one's friends. You are my friends if you do what I command you" (Jn 15:13-14). Here Jesus is holding up active doing for another as the basis of friendship. This is the dimension of friendship males are most comfortable with.

But Jesus continues, "I do not call you servants any longer, because the servant does not know what the master is doing; but I have called you friends, because I have made known to you everything that I have heard from my Father" (Jn 15:15). Here Jesus expands the basis of friendship to include confiding in another person. Jesus says that friendship is proved by telling another person everything about oneself. Males are much less comfortable with this dimension of friendship.

Men who become nurturing caretakers of other men may be tempted to rank themselves above the men they are caring for. But Jesus left no room for such a traditional masculine pecking order. After washing his disciples' feet Jesus asked them, "Do you know what I have done to you?" Answering his own question, he says, "I have set you an example, that you also should do as I have done to you. Very truly, I tell you, servants are not greater than their master, nor are messengers greater than the one who sent them. If you know these things, you are blessed if you do them" (Jn 13:12, 15-17).

Jesus gave his disciples a lesson in humility, for normally the task of washing the feet of dinner guests was relegated to slaves. Here we have

Jesus, the guest of honor, dressed like a slave with a towel around his waist, washing the feet of his disciples. We, too, should be servants as we take the responsibility of providing nurture and care not just for women and children but also for other men.

13

FRIENDSHIPS WITH WOMEN
I Want a Sister, Not a Sweetheart

In the pursuit of greater intimacy in their relationships, many men have encountered barriers erected by others, usually by women, usually in the guise of help. It behooves men and women to be conscious of these barriers as they work at getting closer. Perhaps the barrier most frequently mentioned by men is the demand for intimacy. Demanding intimacy invariably arouses a man's defenses and leads to his withdrawal.

MICHAEL MCGILL, *THE MCGILL REPORT ON MALE INTIMACY*

P revious chapters have dealt with a variety of issues that men and women encounter as they attempt to relate to each other—intimacy, power, control, sexuality, spirituality. It seems especially difficult for men to cultivate and maintain intimate yet nonromantic friendships with women. Few men can say, "Some of my closest friends are women." And because of this few women can claim men among their most intimate friends.

Outside of family relationships, an intimate friendship between a man and a woman is rare. I'd like to offer some guidelines men can use in seeking to develop nonromantic yet close relationships with women.

Negotiating Friendship
In early childhood, boys and girls seem to play rather indiscriminately with each other. They have made the basic discovery that anatomy distinguishes boys from girls, but that difference seems minor in light of all the similarities. Girls and boys like to laugh and run and hide and play together. But somewhere along the path of childhood boys and girls begin to huddle in their same-gender groups, finding the other

gender "yucky" and somewhat foreign. In adolescence, this foreignness becomes mysterious and attractive. Young men and young women rediscover the pleasure of each other's company as they are drawn together in friendship, in sexual attraction and sometimes in both.

Many men describe their wives as their best friend. Some couples came to be friends first while single, only to experience the growth of physical and romantic attraction between them. Other couples were first strongly attracted to each other physically, and then became friends as they discovered similar values and interests and the comfort of companionship.

When men and women come together as friends, they cannot do so as neuter beings. They bring their whole selves, including their maleness and femaleness—their sexuality. They bring to the relationship their needs and desires and their abilities to communicate, choose and set limits.

In friendships that develop between single men and women, the question whether their relationship will be platonic or romantic may be left open. Sometimes the same things that attract friends—shared interests, ability to have fun, comfort in each other's presence—are what attract lovers. In the early stages of a relationship between a man and a woman, they may feel a bit uncertain about how the relationship will develop. They may date and find they would rather be friends. They may enjoy each other but have no inclination to date.

When either friend is married to someone else, the options are removed. They must come together in friendship, understanding that their relationship will not be sexual, or they must not come together at all. This does not lessen the potential for sexual feelings between them, but the marriage bond determines the limits of all other friendships.

Even when men and women have become friends without any wishes for romantic involvement, sexuality is an underlying issue. The fact that they recognize each other as man and woman highlights the interweaving of our sexuality and our personhood. Men and women who become close friends cope with the sexual issues in a variety of ways. Some operate with unspoken rules about what is appropriate in an opposite-gender friendship. Others proceed with their friendship, but it breaks down when one or the other becomes frightened by sexual feelings and attempt to lessen the threat through avoidance.

The Avoidance Strategy

Mark and Sue were neighbors in the same apartment complex. One day at the pool, they noticed that they were both reading the same book, and they began to discuss it. Quickly discovering that they had much else in common, they began meeting fairly regularly at the pool and the tennis court. They both had demanding jobs and were not involved in exclusive dating relationships, so their developing friendship was an important source of companionship. They teased each other easily and discussed their current love interests at length. Though she found acceptance and safety in her friendship with Mark, Sue didn't feel that "chemistry" she knew from romantic relationships.

One night Mark met Sue at the door with a bouquet of flowers. Because of some of his recent comments, Sue thought he might be feeling attracted to her. She didn't want to hurt his feelings by her desire to remain "just friends," nor did she want to lose his friendship. But she started going to the pool less and spending more time with other friends. When Mark called, she was polite but distant. He soon called less.

While being married should provide the clear boundaries needed for the development of opposite-gender friendships, avoidance is still common. Paul and Tonya Irwin were in their thirties, had a fairly healthy marriage and had three school-age children. Jerry and Carolyn Jordan were neighbors who lived down the block. They were also in their thirties and had two children, and their marriage was basically sound, with only the typical types of disagreements.

After Paul and Tonya invited the Jordans over for a backyard barbecue, their families hit it off together. They spent time in each other's homes numerous times and even went on a vacation together to the beach.

The families enjoyed each other immensely, and there was a great deal of teasing whenever they got together. Tonya and Jerry especially found that their senses of humor were compatible. Paul, although good-natured, was a more serious type than Jerry.

While Tonya was deeply in love with her husband, Paul, she had to admit to herself that she really liked the way Jerry teased her, and she appreciated his enthusiastic approach to life. In fact, she found herself quite attracted to Jerry and flirtatiously sought out his attention. She believed that he might be attracted to her also.

Tonya's feelings and flirtatious behavior began to bother her, making her feel guilty and frightened. Could she be falling in love with another man? She was sure of her love for Paul, so she didn't understand the attraction she was feeling for Jerry.

One day Paul suggested to Tonya that they ask Jerry and Carolyn to go with them to a movie. Tonya surprised herself when she suggested that maybe they should get to know Steve and Julie Anderson better, and should ask them instead.

From this point on, the Irwins and Jordans saw less and less of each other, since Tonya usually found some excuse why they could not be together. She never did talk to Paul about her attraction for Jerry, and she most certainly did not discuss the situation with Jerry and Carolyn. She handled her attraction for Jerry by simply avoiding contact with him.

Avoidance is one way out of the dilemma, but it also involves a cost. In this case, it cost the Irwins and Jordans a close relationship with each other. Suppose the same thing were to occur in Paul and Tonya's relationship with Steve and Julie. Has Tonya established a pattern whereby, when she feels confusion and guilt, she will just avoid the situation associated with those feelings? Is she developing a pattern of not sharing her confusing feelings with anyone?

Avoidance or withdrawal is a common way for many people to escape from a situation of potential conflict, and usually the avoider does not share the conflict or problem with another person. Some cultures use avoidance as a way of preventing any close friendships between members of the opposite sex. In the Near East, conservative Muslim societies traditionally have allowed no opposite-sex friendships beyond the immediate family. A man can expect to be close to only his mother, his sister and his wife. A woman can expect to have friendships with no men except her father, her brother and her husband. Women wear body-covering veils in public to prevent any nonfamilial intimacy between men and women.

Muslim societies even differentiate space by sex. There is male space and female space. Any public area—the marketplace, roads, squares and sidewalks—is male space. A female is forbidden to enter male space alone; she must either be with a group of women or be escorted by her husband, father or brother. Private space is female space, and is usually defined within the walls of a home. Males are not allowed to enter this female space unless a father, husband or brother is present.

There are very few extramarital physical exchanges between adult men and women in most Muslim societies. But, needless to say, there are also very few close opposite-sex friendships in these societies. By contrast, in the United States there is ample opportunity for opposite-sex friendships—so much that some would argue that this freedom has caused many problems in our society. Yet I hold to the ideal that close opposite-sex friendships are both possible and desirable. The question is, how can these friendships be established?

Guidelines for Male-Female Friendship

Ronda is a therapist working for the Forest City Counseling Center. She is happily married to her husband, Ben, and they have three children. Brent also works at the counseling center, and he and Ronda often counsel together. Brent has been happily married to his wife, Nancy, for eight years. Although Ronda and Brent are both committed to their spouses, they spend much time together at the center and have grown very close. They enjoy working together, appreciate the intellectual stimulation they share and find each other physically attractive.

The above fictitious example is similar to the situation in which many men and women are finding themselves. Women today make up over one-third of the labor force, and the contact between opposite-gender married persons is greater than it has ever been.

An increasing reason for divorce in the United States is that one spouse wants the freedom to marry someone else. One obvious protection from this danger is not to allow oneself to become close to members of the opposite gender. But this solution rejects any emotional content in a relationship, and it means losing the possibility for some meaningful and wholesome friendships.

An alternative to closing off growth in an opposite-gender friendship is to follow certain guidelines as the friendship develops. To begin with, we need to realize that there are several levels on which a friendship between a man and a woman can operate. In the marriage relationship, the husband and wife share themselves with each other on every level—intellectual, emotional, physical. Other friendships cannot encompass all these levels.

I believe a close opposite-gender friendship is possible when the following principles are practiced.

First, the relationship can involve intellectual, emotional and psychological intimacy, but only limited physical intimacy.

Second, commitment will be given to the relationship as long as it remains nonthreatening and secondary to the marital relationships.

Forms of Intimacy
Physical closeness. Upon experiencing sexual attraction and desire for a friend, your first reaction may be to deny the feelings because of the guilt and confusion they cause. Denial of feelings, however, is not a good solution, and ultimately denial can have only harmful consequences to yourself, your friendship and your marriage.

I believe that there are very few close male-female friendships in which physical attraction does not crop up at least occasionally. When this occurs, the first thing to do is admit the feelings and be openly aware of what is happening. The feelings themselves are not the problem, but rather how you decide to handle them. They can be contained or acted on.

What is the best way to contain sexual feelings in a friendship? First, verbalize your feelings to yourself and to your spouse. Doing this releases any sense of guilt that might be associated with the feelings and with denying that they are present. It also creates an atmosphere of trust and openness. But most of all, it establishes a basis for finding some guidelines in the friendship.

It is hard to overemphasize the importance of this stage in a friendship with someone of the opposite gender. I believe that unless opposite-gender friends clearly establish guidelines when feelings of attraction first become an issue, they are likely either to withdraw from each other or to rationalize their relationship until they become physically involved.

The responsibility for establishing guidelines in a male-female friendship rests with both friends. Not only will they discuss the guidelines together, but they will also freely discuss them with both their spouses. A few possible guidelines follow.

First, it's important that the friends and their spouses not assume anything. Instead, impressions and plans should always be checked out with the others. As an example, Ronda and Brent may both be planning to attend a state counseling convention in a neighboring city. Attendance involves spending two nights at the convention site. It would be easy to assume that they would drive together to the conference. But this assumption should be checked out with each other and with each spouse.

Second, both friends should assume responsibility for any physical contact between them. As I pointed out in chapter eight, traditional expectations are that the man will be the sexual aggressor and the woman the one who sets the limits. This is part of the double standard that excuses sexual promiscuity in males and condemns it in females. This standard is inherently contradictory and hypocritical. Both the man and the woman will control the physical limits in a healthy opposite-gender friendship.

Third, neither friend will be sexually flirtatious. There are numerous ways in which to flirt and tease sexually. Given the extent to which sexual teasing is used in advertising and the mass media, by the time American youth graduate from high school most have mastered the art. Sexual teasing can take the form of tight or revealing clothes, a come-hither smile, an off-color joke, a sexual pun and the like.

Most of us are conscious of our sexual teasing and flirtatious actions. If, however, an innocent gesture is being wrongly interpreted as a sexual tease, this should be brought to the attention of the friend. Some persons are able to touch others very naturally, free of any sexual connotation. Others, who have been reared in restrictive backgrounds, may feel uncomfortable with such touching. To them, touching may have sexual connotations. Such differences are be expected and must be discussed openly.

Fourth, the friendship should always follow the lead of the person with the strongest felt limits. Take the area of touch. If Ronda feels perfectly free and innocent in giving a friendly hug, but Brent does not, they will agree to abide by Brent's limits. Or it may be that Ronda and Brent are contemplating driving together to a distant counseling convention which requires an overnight stop on the way. Although they would have separate rooms in the motel, Ronda feels uncomfortable about the arrangement. In this case Brent will respect Ronda's limits.

It goes without saying that married spouses will have full knowledge of any such arrangements and be in full accord. It may be that both Ronda and Brent feel comfortable with the traveling arrangement, but either Ronda's or Brent's spouse is not very enthusiastic about it. Then Ronda and Brent will accept the limits of their spouses without any feelings of resentment or curtailment. Not all situations will be as delicate as this one, but the guidelines can be applied in the same way.

Intellectual sharing. One of the most unrealistic and unnecessary burdens we have placed upon the modern marriage relationship is the expectation that our spouse will fulfill all our needs. Too often we expect our husband or wife to be all things to us. The result is that the spouse feels inadequate when he or she can't meet all of our needs. A further result is jealousy when someone else is better able to fulfill just one dimension of our spouse's needs.

Today each employed spouse is likely to be involved in a very specialized form of work. In the past, when the majority of families were agricultural, husband and wife were involved in the same type of economic activity. But today, husbands and wives often have very little direct knowledge of the details of their spouse's occupation. Because of occupational specialization, then, a high degree of intellectual sharing is possible in opposite-gender friendships.

It is within our occupational tasks that many of our creative energies are expressed. We admire and are drawn to others in our field who possess creative energies similar to our own. With the increased partic-

ipation of women in all levels of employment, opposite-gender friendships can be expected to develop on this basis.

Ronda, although a good counselor, may really admire the way Brent
is able to conduct group counseling. She specializes in individual counseling, and Brent has a real admiration for her skills in this area. As they
spend time at coffee breaks and over lunch talking about counseling
theories and techniques, they may develop a mutual admiration and
understanding on an intellectual level—an understanding that is not as
fully developed with their spouses. Is there anything dangerous or undesirable about this?

The degree of intellectual intimacy that can develop between opposite-gender friends is dependent upon the strength and health of the
relationship between each friend and his and her spouse. If Ronda's
husband happens to be a successful lawyer who is quite secure in his
occupation and intellectual ability, he will likely be delighted in Ronda's
intellectual intimacy with Brent. On the other hand, if he is really struggling professionally and is unsure of his intellectual ability, he may very
well be resentful of the positive affirmation Brent is receiving from
Ronda.

I am not suggesting that each spouse must be intellectually fulfilled
by the other spouse in some academic way before they can tolerate any
intellectual closeness with others. Suppose that Brent's wife completed
her high-school education and then became a secretary before she met
and married Brent. She now has three children and is a busy homemaker, but still finds time to lead a Girl Scout troop and teach the eighth-
grade Sunday-school class at church. She is creative in all her tasks and
is receiving much positive reinforcement from others. She is secure
enough in herself intellectually that she can encourage Brent in his
intellectual intimacy with Ronda. If the marriage relationships are secure, I see no limits in the intellectual intimacy that can develop between opposite-gender friends.

Emotional intimacy. Emotional intimacy is the psychological and social dimension of a friendship. As two people come to feel emotionally
comfortable with each other, emotional intimacy is experienced as total
acceptance of the other, free from demands or expectations for change.

Friends will be free to express their feelings to each other.

Again, however, the extent to which opposite-gender married friends can become emotionally intimate will depend upon the nature of their marriage relationships. Ronda and Brent are counselors who are skilled in the art of human relating. They have developed empathic skills, are trained to be sensitive to others' needs and feelings and know when and how to say a comforting or challenging word. If this is true, then isn't it possible that Ronda and Brent could establishing a more intimate emotional relationship with each other than either is able to establish with his or her spouse? Yes, this may be a very real possibility, and it might become a danger to the marriage relationship. This danger is dealt with in the second principle of opposite-gender friendships.

Male-Female Friendships and Marriage

My second principle for male-female friendships states that commitment will be given to the friendship as long as it remains nonthreatening and secondary to the primary marital relationship of each friend. This principle has been implied throughout my discussion of the first principle—that physical, intellectual and emotional intimacy must be highly developed in both friends' marriage relationships before intimacy can develop in the friendship. If intimacy were to be greater between the friends than in either's marriage, there would be a real danger that the marriage would become secondary.

Male-female friendships must always remain secondary to marriage. The friends need to keep in touch with their own psychological needs and wants. They must be so secure in themselves and in their marriages that they will not allow the friendship to become primary.

If a spouse is not receiving sufficient emotional intimacy, if basic psychological and social needs are not being met in the marriage, then the development of an intimate opposite-gender friendship can be dangerous. A decision at this point should involve limiting the friendship and working to build a stronger marriage.

Close friendships between men and women are wonderful. They can provide rich experiences and serve to strengthen the marriage relationship. But married persons should be open to developing such friendships only if they already are a part of a loving, meaningful, intimate marriage relationship.

Should male-female friendships be avoided simply because you recognize that your marriage has shortcomings? No, certainly not. But be aware of your vulnerability when the friendship promises to become more intimate than the marriage.

Till Inconvenience Do Us Part

Men who are fortunate enough to have a close friendship with a woman must not get a false sense of their permanence. When you marry, you commit yourself to your spouse for life—till death parts you. Your commitment to your friend, though, will continue only as long as it works and positively contributes to your marriage relationship. The friendship can end when one friend moves away, finds another job or changes in ways that the other can't tolerate.

Giving up an intimate friendship is not easy. It may not always be necessary, but sometimes you will need to give up being close to your friend. Then you should view the intimacy of friendship as a positive force that has caused personal growth and prepared you to establish other intimate friendships in the future.

Rich Marriage, Rich Friendships

As I grew up, I was very much an inexpressive male. During my high-school and college days I found it hard to relate closely to females. In early high school I was apt to be a big tease—playfully pretending to steal a book away from girls, splashing water on them at the swimming pool or mocking and taunting them between classes. Toward the end of high school, I became the strong, silent type. With my deep involvement in sports, I pretended that I didn't have time for girls, when in fact I was rather scared and uncomfortable at the thought of asking a girl for a date.

I continued in this mode during my first year in college. But as I gained success on the college basketball team, I gradually became brave enough to ask women out. Although I soon found myself quite popular with both women and men, I still found it difficult to talk freely with women.

During my sophomore year I met Judy, the woman who was to become my wife. She was a cheerleader, so we had a common interest in sports, and it seemed only natural to ask her out.

I soon found that Judy was a little different from most of the women I had known. She seemed to be genuinely interested in what I had to say. She was free to talk about her feelings, and she asked me how I felt about things in nonthreatening ways. Judy was the first woman with whom I was able to establish a close, intimate relationship.

As our relationship has grown over the years, my ability to establish opposite-gender friendships has also developed. Let me tell you about my friendship with a woman I'll call Jill (although I'm sure neither she nor her husband would object to being identified in this book; both in fact have read what follows).

I first met Jill when she was an undergraduate student at a college where I was teaching. She was intelligent and creative, the type of student who makes teaching rewarding. From the beginning, Judy knew of my enthusiasm for Jill's ability. I was delighted that Jill wanted to become a sociologist. She became a very close friend to both Judy and me.

Between Jill's junior and senior years, I left the college to teach at the University of Georgia. I continued to correspond with Jill and advised her on applying to graduate programs. Due to her outstanding undergraduate record, Jill was accepted by a number of graduate sociology programs. As it turned out, she decided to come to the University of Georgia.

Although Jill renewed her friendship with Judy and me after she arrived in Georgia, she soon began to question her purpose in life and the meaning of her existence. At the height of the student countercultural movement, Jill experimented with drugs and Eastern mysticism. Once I answered the phone in the middle of the night. It was Jill, crying in desperate loneliness and fear, under the effects of drugs. I went to get her and brought her back to our home, where Judy and I comforted her until she could go to sleep.

One day Jill came into my office at school and began to cry, telling me how confused she felt as to what life was all about. I felt very inadequate at the time. As I remember, I told her that I believed life's meaning was centered in a personal relationship with Jesus Christ. I then assured her that God really loved her, and that I too loved her. I shed tears with her, because I cared about the loneliness and turmoil she was experiencing.

Through her personal searching and reading of the Bible, Jill came into a relationship with Jesus Christ. Uncertain of the implications of her newfound faith, she didn't tell me about her decision until two months after she'd made it.

With both of us committed to the lordship of Jesus Christ, our relationship proceeded on a firmer foundation. She and I had a special relationship. Perhaps I was in part a father substitute (her father had died when she was very young). It was important for her to feel loved by me as a man and also to grapple with difficult questions about life's meaning and the relationship between Christianity and sociology. The relationship was important to me too, because it was proving to me that I could be in an intimate friendship with a woman other than my wife. The relationship did not threaten my marriage, because Jill also felt close to Judy and to us as a couple.

Jill now has her doctoral degree and is a college sociology professor. She is also married and the mother of two children. Jill's husband, Rick, is a very warm, expressive person, more than I am, and I count him as one of my very closest male friends. Judy is as close to Rick as I am to Jill and counts herself equally close to both Rick and Jill.

As I think about the degree of closeness the four of us have been able to achieve, it seems to me the key has been that each of us is first of all committed to the lordship of Christ. Second, we are committed to our spouses and the primacy of our marriage relationships. And third, we are committed to each other as persons, based upon the strength of the first two commitments.

PART V

CONCLUSION

14

MEN MADE NEW

Beyond Traditional Roles and Modern Options

As we who are men increasingly become part of this [change] process, we will become better lovers. We will become better friends of God, of our world, and of ourselves. We will know in a new way that the Word continues to become flesh and dwell among and within us. And as that happens, our male energy will be more life-giving than we have yet known.

JAMES NELSON, *THE INTIMATE CONNECTION*

T he current change in gender roles is a process that has altered the very identity of women and men. As this change disrupts many aspects of their personal, family and social lives, men have understandably reacted with confusion, discouragement and anger. I have argued in this book that men need to see this disruption as an opportunity to reexamine the traditional definition of manhood in the light of biblical principles.

I have noted two unhelpful reactions Christian men might take. One is to react negatively and defensively to all changes and attempt to restore gender roles to what they were in an idealized past. These efforts are based on the fallacy that the traditional patriarchal system represents the biblical ideal for society today. This approach ignores the complexity of the issues and overlooks the unbiblical and harmful aspects of the traditional gender-role system.

A second unhelpful reaction consists of simply welcoming all new definitions of masculinity as they are introduced. I have pointed out how some of these attempts are based on naturalistic and relativistic assumptions. While avoiding the pitfalls of idealizing particular cultural definitions, those who uncritically welcome change fail to acknowledge any normative base for defining masculinity.

In this book I have attempted to demonstrate how a Christian model of masculinity might deal with the most problematic contemporary male issues—intimacy and emotional expressiveness, war and competition, power and control, sexuality, spirituality, life-cycle stages and interpersonal relationships. This last chapter will offer some practical suggestions on *how* men can change, address women who would like to help men change and end with an appeal to Christian men to live out their values and beliefs in *community*.

Practical Ways to Facilitate Change

If a man wants to change, how can he begin? First, let me point out that most of us have already changed more than we think. Only a hermit could be unaffected by the reexamination of gender roles that has occurred during the last twenty years. But the way we change needs to be intentional, based upon Christian conviction rather than merely external social pressures.

If some of the ideas presented in this book make sense, I urge you to put your beliefs and convictions about manhood into action. Suggested below are a number of activities that might facilitate your journey toward a more authentic manhood. Some of the suggested activities, such as attending a men's conference or keeping a "gender journal," do not require a major time commitment; others, such as joining a men's group, will demand a greater commitment but may also bring wonderful rewards.

Attend a men's conference. A number of churches and parachurch organizations are offering men's conferences that deal with a variety of issues facing men today. Attending such a conference can be an affirming but nonthreatening way for you to reflect on some of the issues raised in this book. By including small-group discussions along with lectures, such conferences allow you to share your concerns and experiences with other men.

Keep a gender journal. Keeping a "gender journal" simply involves entering information into a notebook each week:

1. Record the incidents that caused you to experience your strongest feelings during the week.

2. Note the types of feelings these incidents brought about—love, joy, happiness, elation, fear, resentment, anger, etc.

3. Note the incidents that made you glad you are a male.

4. Note the incidents that made you wish you were not a male.

5. Note the relationships in which you felt the most supported.

6. Note the relationships in which you feel you were most supportive of another.

Feel free to delete from or add to this list, depending upon the issues that currently concern you most as a male.

Write a personal history. You may begin with how you think your mother and father reacted upon learning that you were a boy. Were they glad? Disappointed?

What sort of a boy were you in your early youth? Were you athletic? A good student? Well liked by the other boys? Were you self-confident?

As you grew older, did you have any fears or insecurities around other boys? Around girls? What were your feelings about being a male when you became a teenager? Were you proud or embarrassed about your physique? Who were your male heroes—the men you looked up to and most wanted to be like? What do you think the girls thought of you? Were girls eager to date you?

What were your greatest anticipations and fears when you stopped living at home? When you left home, how would you describe your relationship with your father? With your mother?

These questions are merely suggestive; the important thing is for you to record the thoughts and feelings you experienced growing up as a male.

Reflect on Jesus as a man. Reflect on what the Gospels tell us about the life of Jesus by making a list of words you would use to characterize Jesus. When you have done this, go over the list of words you have developed, and use traditional gender-role stereotypes to categorize each word as either "masculine," "feminine" or "neither." Next, add up the words within each category. How would Jesus be regarded as a man in our society?

Ask your father about his relationship with his father. Perhaps you, like many other men, have little understanding of how your father views his relationship with his father. With a little encouragement, most fathers welcome the chance to share their views with their sons.

Begin your questions in a nonthreatening, general way—"What did you do for fun when you were growing up, Dad?" or "What did you like best about growing up where you did?" After you sense a willingness in your father to talk about his past, you might ease into a more direct style of questioning: "What was your favorite thing to do with Grandfather?" or "Dad, what was Grandfather like as a father to you?"

If you sense continued openness to share, you can follow up with any number of more specific questions: "Did Grandfather play with you often?" "Did he ever share with you how it was for him growing up?" "Did he show an interest in your schoolwork, sports or hobbies?" "What is the warmest memory you have about your relationship with him?"

You need to be sensitive to your father. He may never have verbalized some of the feelings and memories your questions will provoke. But I've found that when asked, fathers share much more with their grown sons than the sons expected.

See a movie with male friends. Invite several of your male friends to watch one of the following videos with you: *Bang the Drum Slowly, City Slickers, The Deer Hunter, Diner, Dominick and Eugene, The Great Santini, Kramer vs. Kramer, The Last Detail, The Last Picture Show, M*A*S*H, The Man Who Would Be King, One Flew Over the Cuckoo's Nest, Ordinary People, Patton, Platoon, The Right Stuff, Tender Mercies* or *Tin Men.*

I have suggested these films because each deals with an important aspect of masculinity. After viewing the film, share your thoughts about the image of masculinity projected by the main male characters in the film. What aspects of masculinity were you drawn to? What aspects of masculinity were repulsive to you?

Join a men's group. I have found that one of the best things men can do for themselves in this time of gender-role confusion is to become a part of a men's group. Although the emphases can vary, the basic purpose of a men's group is to provide a place where men can be a support to each other while sharing personal experiences and discussing common concerns.

The ideal size of a men's group is between four and eight, and the group should meet from one to two hours each week or every other week. Although there can be much diversity in age, socioeconomic status, ethnicity, education and so on, in general, the more similar men are in life experience, the more likely it is that they will establish deep and trusting relationships with each other. Yet diversity can also be a strength: one of my most meaningful experiences was in a men's group that had a forty-year age range. Similar life experiences will not be as important as the willingness on the part of *all* men in the group to be honest and open with one another.

Although it usually takes the efforts of one or two men to start a group, once the group is under way leadership can be shared. There are a few important rules that every successful men's group needs to follow:

1. Each member will make a commitment to be at every meeting unless prevented by sickness or travel.

2. Anything that is said in the group is completely confidential and cannot be shared outside of the group without the group's permission.

3. Every group member must assume responsibility for the group's becoming what it needs to be to meet his needs. This means being willing to share concerns, request help and support, and confront others where necessary.

Group meetings can focus upon predetermined topics or can be left unstructured. I have found that it is good to begin a meeting by allowing members to share what has been going on in their lives the previous week. This can be followed by discussion centered on any one of a variety of topics (see the previous chapter titles and section headings for examples). Any of the individual exercises described above—gender journals, personal gender histories, reflections on Jesus as a man and exploring relationships with fathers—can also serve as the basis for discussion in a men's group.

An entire meeting may need to be devoted to an issue raised by one member during the sharing time. A group needs to be flexible enough to allow for this, and not held captive to a predetermined schedule of topics. A successful men's group will need to be self-monitoring in balancing its needs for flexibility and structure.

Wandering from topic to topic within a given meeting will not be as fruitful as focusing in depth on one topic. If, for example, the relationship with one's father is the topic of discussion, the following types of questions might be interjected into the discussion: What was your relationship like with your father as you were growing up? How did he express his love for you? His anger toward you? How did you know that he was proud of you? Describe the times when you felt closest to your father. How would you describe your relationship with your father now? If you could ask your father anything and be sure that he would give you an honest answer, what would it be? How would you like your relationship with your father to be different from what it is now?

I can't stress it strongly enough: *Men who are at the crossroads of masculine concerns need the support of a men's group.* The rewards can be tremendous and life-changing.

Can Women Help Men Change?

During the 1970s, women came to the conclusion that their movement must be for women and *by* women. Men who were sympathetic to women's causes were told that they need not join the women's movement, but instead had their work cut out for them in raising the consciousness of *men.* As this is increasingly happening, it is legitimate to ask whether women can play a role in the men's movement. My answer is no; men need to work through their masculinity issues in the same way that women are dealing with issues of femininity.

But this doesn't mean that women can't or shouldn't be involved on a *personal* level with men who are struggling with masculinity issues. Women in committed relationships with men, especially in marriage, can be effective in helping men through their struggle with gender issues.

A woman can help a man change. But first, she must tell herself not to become fatalistic about the situation.

A woman grows up in a family with a controlling, uncommunicative father. Her mother tells her, "That's the way men are." When she marries, she believes that her husband is different. But time passes, and she concludes her mother was right after all—that men are insensitive, controlling and inexpressive. She resigns herself to living with a husband whose personal characteristics serve as barriers to a richer marriage relationship. But she shouldn't.

Helping him to talk. A wife can begin to help an inexpressive husband to realize how much he has shut off his feelings by saying something like this: "I'd really be interested to know what's going on at work— you seldom tell me anything about it." (It is amazing, as studies show, how many wives have only the vaguest notion of what their husbands do for a living.) Or she can say, "You've never told me how it was when you were a kid."

Of course, she shouldn't make her request a challenge or reproach. She must be genuinely interested in knowing about what concerns him—as indeed most wives are.

By opening up an area a man is fairly comfortable with—his youth, his work, his hobby—and then asking him how he felt or feels about it, a woman will find it easier to lead him into more open conversations. It may be fairly easy for a man to tell a woman what he does at work; it is going to be much harder for him to say whether he enjoys his work or is bored with it, but that is really what is crucial to communication between a man and a woman. Similarly, he may be able to say fairly easily that he used to play football every afternoon after school on the corner lot; it will be a lot harder for him to say he felt miserable because he wasn't very good at it, or describe the thrill he felt the time he caught a touchdown pass. But again, his feelings are the crucial matter.

I suggest, then, that from time to time a wife try her husband on such straightforward topics. If he shrugs her off with a noncommittal answer—"I don't mind my work"—she might try once more—"But you seem discouraged lately, and I wondered if something at work was bothering you." If he remains noncommittal, she's probably best advised not to press him, but to bide her time.

A key is for the wife to open her heart when her husband is offering to share some of his feelings. She may not always think he's right; she may think he shouldn't have felt so angry when his boss criticized his work, or when his father gave his brother an old car. But if she wants him to communicate with her, she must show empathy. I don't mean that a wife should play up to her husband and simply agree with everything he says; but it is usually wise to temper the truth with compassion.

A woman doesn't have to agree with a man's viewpoint to empathize with his feelings. Suppose a man has had a disagreement with a friend or relative—his father, for example. He says angrily, "I can't get anything through his thick head." A wife may feel that they're both wrong, but the important thing is for her to support her husband. She might say, "I know you're really angry right now; I wonder what's making you so mad?"

Once she has gotten him to vent his feelings on the subject, it may then be time for her to say, "I understand what you're feeling; I'm wondering if you've thought about. . . ." This may provide him with a different viewpoint of the situation and will help him reach a solution. She may go on, "I want you to know how much it means to me that you're sharing this with me. Right now I have mixed feelings about the situation, but I hope it's helpful to talk it out this way."

This is what psychologists call "positive reinforcement." The man is being rewarded—in this case with his wife's appreciation—for his openness, and this inevitably encourages him to repeat it. It may sometimes be difficult for the wife to be supportive of her husband's efforts to be more communicative, especially when he expresses troublesome feelings about his job, family or other matters that are important to her; but she should try to remember that she can always go over the ground again later. The immediate point is to encourage him to keep talking.

Change comes from within. I have two reservations about encouraging women to help men change. First, men have traditionally depended upon women to do their "emotional work" for them. It would be unfair to dump an extra load upon a woman who is already overloaded and struggling to define who she is as a woman. As men and women seek to understand and help each other, they need to become aware of how rigid definitions of gender roles have kept them in codependent relationships with each other. The key is for men and women to support each other in ways that will empower them to overcome the barriers placed upon them by traditional views of masculinity and femininity. A careful reading of the above section will, I hope, reveal relational principles that work toward empowerment rather than dependence.

Second, I have perhaps made it seem as if it were a wife's job to change her husband. This, of course, is not true. A wife can *help*. She can help her husband see how his acquired view of masculinity has limited him in his relationships. But change must come from within us males.

As I begin to get angry because my teenage son has beaten me at a one-on-one game of basketball, I might ask myself if this is the response of a mature male. If I don't like the way I'm responding, I can make a beginning by complimenting and congratulating my son for becoming such a fine player. Then I may come to feel good when my son beats me, because it is evidence that I have taught him well! I can experience the true liberation that comes when I no longer feel that I must compete with my children, but can share in the triumphs of their successes because I have empowered them.

If I recognize myself as the "strong, silent type," I might ask whether I would rather be more open and expressive of my love for my wife and children. If my answer is yes, then I can make a beginning by simply trying to talk more often about what I *really feel.*

I know from personal experience that it isn't easy. It was very hard for me at first to begin to tell my wife that I cared for her, to say that I loved her, to share my feelings. But I did, and the rewards have been enormous. Not only has my marriage been enriched and my relationships with my children deepened, but the change has spread through my whole life. Because I am willing to let people see who I am in my strengths and weaknesses, I have become a better teacher, a better friend, even a better scholar. For after all, one of the jobs of a sociologist is to learn about people, and how can you ask people to tell you who they are if you aren't willing to tell them who you are in return?

Men in Christian Community
I have written this book with the conviction that the model of manhood

offered within Christianity is desperately needed in the modern world. Although this model needs to be articulated well, attempts to do so will be ineffective unless Christian men effectively live out their values and beliefs in Christian community.

It was said of the early church that people knew they were Christians because of the love they showed for one another. So it needs to be with Christian men: we will know that their masculinity is authentic by the way they love others in Christian community. This is especially true because of men's propensity to dominate, control and lord it over others. What better way to gauge true Christian manhood than to examine how men relate to their brothers and sisters in the faith?

The signs of authentic Christian masculinity will be that men in Christian community will seek to *support rather than dominate women, empower rather than control younger men* and *mentor and complement rather than compete with other men.*

Men supporting women. A danger in a book focusing upon male issues is the appearance of being insensitive to the needs of women. Men who are seeking to be authentic followers of Jesus will recognize that Christian men have all too often participated in oppressing and discriminating against women. We must repent for any part we might have in these practices and affirm our support for full Christian womanhood.

The Bible clearly calls all believers to fight against oppression and discrimination, and this is no less true when the oppressed are women. Men's attempt to be liberated from an internal emotional straitjacket must go hand in hand with attempts to liberate women from external social structures that have kept them in bondage. There can be no true men's liberation without a women's liberation, and vice versa.

Secure Christian manhood means that one is so mature that he need not confirm his masculinity at a woman's expense. Such a man will be secure enough not only to work with a woman as an equal but also to learn from a woman, and even to work under her supervision. The world will recognize the authenticity of Christian manhood when it sees Christian men who support rather than oppress women.

Men empowering younger men. The initiation of boys into manhood by men, a nearly universal practice in nonindustrial societies, has all but disappeared in modern industrial society. As I pointed out in chapter ten, teenage boys in our society experience stress and strain as they struggle to achieve manhood without guidance from a community of caring men. Where attempts at initiation into manhood do occur, it involves older boys' trying to initiate younger boys into youth gangs.

As Robert Bly rightly points out, it takes a *community* of men to effectively initiate boys into manhood. Men in Christian community can demonstrate their manly love by actively initiating boys into manhood. A Jewish tradition, the bar mitzvah, is an example of how a community of faith can provide for boys' initiation.

A few years ago I attended the bar mitzvah of the son of a Jewish friend. The young man, who had spent several years studying Hebrew under the tutelage of a rabbi, was guided in his bar mitzvah by the men in the community. After reading a portion of the Torah in Hebrew, the young man gave a short speech. I was struck by his concluding sentence: "And now I am a man!"

This is precisely what the Christian community of men needs to be providing for younger men. Initiation into manhood can't be done by the boy's mother or father, although they can be supportive. Young men need to be initiated by a *community of men*. There is a strength in a community of men that can empower young men as nothing else can.

To be effective, the men must model love by showing their *supreme concern* for the boys in the community. It is from the community of men that a boy can obtain his mature masculine identity. While an effective Christian initiation might include a ritual similar to the bar mitzvah, it must also include a community of men who actively practice their love by respecting, affirming, knowing, giving themselves to, caring for and being responsible for the boys in their community.

The self-doubt and confusion within adolescent boys today are so great that nothing short of a radical display of love by men in Christian community can heal the wounds. Men in Christian community have a tremendous opportunity to demonstrate the authenticity of their radical Christian love by initiating boys into manhood.

Men mentoring and complementing other men. When boys become

young men, they continue to need the acceptance, affirmation and
guidance of older men. They need mentoring!

As I noted in chapter twelve, a true mentor is one who not only passes
on wisdom and knowledge but also takes responsibility for the total
well-being of the novice. A man who is a mentor needs to provide
supportive security which will be experienced by the younger man as
an "emotional holding."

In biblical terms, mentoring is men *discipling* younger men. In his
relationship with his disciples, Jesus modeled how a mentor can care
for a disciple. (See the last section of chapter twelve for a fuller discussion of Jesus as the model of a nurturing caretaker.) Men in Christian
community need to be intentional in developing nurturing relationships
with younger men. Young men, for their part, need to seek out older
men who can be mentors to them. The development of such relationships within the Christian community would be a magnificent witness
to the power of Christian manhood.

Finally, men in the Christian community need to make a radical break
with the usual way men behave in social organizations. We need to be
a living example of the body of Christ as described in 1 Corinthians 12.
Instead of competing with each other, we need to experience the affirmation of being in a complementary unity with one another. Each of
us need to experience being a vital part of a united body in which he
nurtures and is nourished.

What a witness for Christian masculinity it would be if men in Christian community exemplified such unity! It's my prayer that Christian
men will be released from the bondage of a traditional masculine model, protected from the false aspects of modern models and allowed to
experience the authentic fullness of manhood as modeled by Jesus
Christ.

References

Anderson, R. 1982. *On Being Human: Essays in Theological Anthropology*. Grand Rapids, Mich.: Eerdmans.

Balswick, J. O. 1978. *Why I Can't Say I Love You*. Waco, Tex.: Word Books.

Balswick, J. O. 1988. *The Inexpressive Male*. Lexington, Mass.: Lexington Books.

Balswick, J. O., and J. K. Balswick. 1987. "A Theological Basis for Family Relationships." *Journal of Psychology and Christianity* 6:37-49.

Balswick, J. O., and J. K. Balswick. 1990. *The Family: A Christian Perspective on the Contemporary Home*. Grand Rapids, Mich.: Baker Book House.

Balswick, J. O., and K. Morland. 1990. *Social Problems: A Christian Understanding and Response*. Grand Rapids, Mich.: Baker Book House.

Bartchy, S. 1984. "Issues of Power and a Theology of the Family." Address given at The Consultation on a Theology of the Family. Fuller Theological Seminary, Pasadena, Calif.

Baumrind, D. 1967. "Socialization Practices Associated with Dimensions of Social Competence in Preschool Boys and Girls." *Child Development* 38:291-327.

Baumrind, D. 1979. "Current Patterns of Parental Authority." *Developmental Psychology Monographs* 41.

Bell, A., M. Weinberg and S. K. Hammersmith. 1981. *Sexual Preference: Its Development in Men and Women*. Bloomington: Indiana University Press.

Belsky, J., G. Gilstrap and M. Rovine. 1984. "The Pennsylvania Infant and Family Development, Part I: Stability and Change in Mother-Infant and Father-Infant Interaction in a Family Setting at One, Three and Nine Months." *Child De-*

velopment 55:692-705.

Belsky, J., R. Lerner and G. Spanier. 1984. *The Child in the Family.* Reading, Mass.: Addison-Wesley.

Benedict, R. 1938. "Continuities and Discontinuities in Cultural Conditioning." *Psychiatry* 1:161-67.

Berger, B., and P. Berger. 1983. *The War over the Family.* Garden City, N.Y.: Doubleday.

Block, J. 1982. "Assimilation, Accommodation and Dynamics of Personality Development." *Child Development* 53:281-94.

Block, J., J. H. Block and J. Harrington. 1974. "Some Misgivings about the Matching Familiar Figures Test as a Measure of Reflection-Impulsivity." *Developmental Psychology* 10:611-32.

Bly, R. 1990. *Iron John.* Reading, Mass.: Addison-Wesley.

Brod, H. 1987. *The Making of Masculinities: The New Men's Studies.* Boston: Allen & Unwin.

Chartier, M. 1978. "Parenting: A Theological Model." *Journal of Psychology and Theology* 6:54-61.

Chodorow, N. 1978. *The Reproduction of Mothering: Psychoanalysis and the Sociology of Gender.* Berkeley: University of California Press.

Coleman, K. H. 1980. "Conjugal Violence: What Thirty-three Men Report." *Journal of Marital and Family Therapy* 2 (April):7-13.

Dalbey, G. 1988. *Healing the Masculine Soul.* Dallas: Word Books.

David, D. S., and R. Brannon. 1976. *The Forty-nine Percent Majority.* Reading, Mass.: Addison-Wesley.

Dittes, J. 1985. *The Male Predicament: On Being a Man Today.* New York: Harper & Row.

Downey, A. M. 1984. "The Relationship of Sex-Role Orientation to Self-Perceived Health Status in Middle-aged Males." *Sex Roles* 11:211-25.

Ehrensaft, D. 1990. *Parenting Together: Men and Women Sharing the Care of Their Children.* Chicago: University of Illinois Press.

Erikson, E. 1963. *Childhood and Society.* New York: Norton.

Feldman, L. 1990. "Fathers and Fathering," in *Men in Therapy: The Challenge of Change,* ed. R. Meth and R. Pasick. New York: Guilford Press.

Ferguson, A. 1984. "On Conceiving Motherhood and Sexuality: A Feminist Materialist Approach," in *Mothering: Essays in Feminist Theory,* ed. J. Treblicot. Totowa, N.J.: Rowman and Allanheld.

Forward, S., and J. Torres. 1986. *Men Who Hate Women and the Women Who Love Them.* New York: Bantam Books.

Fowler, J. 1981. *Stages of Faith.* New York: Harper & Row.

Franklin, C. 1988. *Men and Society.* Chicago: Nelson-Hall.

Frin, J. 1986. "The Relationship between Sex Role Attitudes and Attitudes Supporting Marital Violence." *Sex Roles* 14:235-44.

Fromm, E. 1956. *The Art of Loving.* New York: Harper & Row.

Garfinkel, P. 1985. *In a Man's World: Father, Son, Brother, Friend and Other Roles Men Play.* New York: Norton.

Gerzon, M. 1982. *A Choice of Heroes: The Changing Face of American Manhood.* Boston: Houghton Mifflin.

Gilligan, C. 1982. *In a Different Voice: Psychological Theory and Women's Development.* Cambridge, Mass.: Harvard University Press.

Gjerde, P. F. 1986. "The Interpersonal Structure of Family Interaction Settings: Parent-Adolescent Relations in Dyads and Triads." *Developmental Psychology* 22:279-304.

Goldberg, H. 1979. *The New Male: From Self-Destruction to Self-Care.* New York: Signet Books.

Harrison, J. 1978. "Warning: The Male Sex Role May Be Dangerous to Your Health." *Journal of Social Issues* 34:66-86.

Hite, S. 1976. *The Hite Report.* New York: Macmillan.

Keen, S. 1991. *Fire in the Belly: On Being a Man.* New York: Bantam Books.

Kinsey, A. 1948. *Sexual Behavior in the Human Male.* Philadelphia: Saunders.

Kinsey, A. 1952. *Sexual Behavior in the Human Female.* Philadelphia: Saunders.

Kirkwood, J. 1973. *P.S., Your Cat Is Dead.* New York: Warner Books.

Kohlberg, L. 1963. "Moral Development and Identification," in *Child Psychology: Sixty-second Yearbook of the National Society for the Study of Education,* ed. H. Stevenson. Chicago: University of Chicago Press.

Korda, M. 1973. *Male Chauvinism: How It Works.* New York: Random House.

Kraybill, D. 1982. *Facing Nuclear War.* Scottdale, Pa.: Herald.

Lamb, M., A. Frodi, C. Hwang, M. Frodi and J. Steinberg. 1982. "Mother and Father-Infant Interaction Involving Play and Holding in Traditional and Non-traditional Swedish Families." *Developmental Psychology* 18:215-21.

Levinson, D. 1978. *The Seasons of a Man's Life.* New York: Ballantine.

Lewis, R. 1978. "Emotional Intimacy among Men." *Journal of Social Issues* 34:108-21.

Lyon, H. 1977. *Tenderness Is Strength: From Machismo to Manhood.* New York: Harper & Row.

McGill, M. 1985. *The McGill Report on Male Intimacy.* New York: Harper & Row.

May, R. 1969. *Love and Will.* New York: Norton.

Moore, R., and D. Gillette. 1990. *King, Warrior, Magician, Lover: Rediscovering the Archetypes of the Mature Masculine.* San Francisco: Harper.

Neal, S. 1978. *The Eisenhowers' Reluctant Dynasty.* Garden City, N.Y.: Doubleday.

Nelson, J. 1988. *The Intimate Connection: Male Sexuality, Masculine Spirituality.* Philadelphia: Westminster Press.

Norwood, R. 1985. *Women Who Love Too Much: When You Keep Wishing and Hoping He'll Change.* New York: Simon & Schuster.

Osherson, S. 1986. *Finding Our Fathers: The Unfinished Business of Manhood.* New York: Free Press.

Oshman, H., and M. Manosevitz. 1976. "Father Absence: Effects of Stepfathers upon Psychosocial Development in Males." *Developmental Psychology* 12:479-80.

Plaskow, J. 1980. *Sex, Sin and Grace: Women's Experience and the Theologies of Reinhold Niebuhr and Paul Tillich.* Lanham, Md.: University Press of America.

Pleck, J. 1980. "Men's Power with Women, Other Men and Society: A Men's Movement Analysis," in *The American Man,* ed. E. Pleck and J. Pleck. Englewood Cliffs, N.J.: Prentice-Hall.

Pleck, J. 1982. *The Myth of Masculinity.* Cambridge, Mass.: MIT Press.

Rekers, G. 1986. "The Family and Gender Identity Disorders." *Journal of Family and Culture* 2(3):8-31.

Ringer, R. 1979. *Winning Through Intimidation.* New York: Fawcett.

Rollins, B., and D. Thomas. 1979. "Parental Support, Power and Control Techniques in the Socialization of Children," in *Contemporary Theories about the Family,* ed. W. Burr, R. Hill, F. Nye and I. Reiss. New York: Free Press.

Rosenbaum, A., and K. D. O'Leary. 1981. "Marital Violence: Characteristics of Abusive Couples." *Journal of Consulting and Clinical Psychology* 4:63-71.

Rossi, A. 1984. "Gender and Parenthood." *American Sociological Review* 49:1-19.

Rubin, L. 1983. *Intimate Strangers: Men and Women Together.* New York: Harper & Row.

Sabo, D., and R. Ross. 1980. *Jock: Sports and Male Identity.* Englewood Cliffs, N.J.: Prentice-Hall.

Sattel, J. 1976. "The Inexpressive Male: Tragedy or Sexual Politics?" *Social Problems* 23:469-77.

Sayers, D. L. 1971. *Are Women Human?* Grand Rapids, Mich.: Eerdmans.

Sheehy, G. 1978. *Passages.* New York: Bantam Books.

Tiger, L. 1969. *Men in Groups.* New York: Random House.

Tiger, L., and R. Fox. 1971. *The Imperial Animal.* New York: Holt, Rinehart & Winston.

Van Leeuwen, M. 1990. *Gender and Grace.* Downers Grove, Ill.: InterVarsity Press.

Wilkinson, R. 1986. *American Tough: The Tough-Guy Tradition and American Character.* New York: Harper & Row.

Wilson, E. 1975. *Sociobiology: The New Synthesis.* Cambridge, Mass.: Belknap/ Harvard University Press.